The Eden Project

Marie-Louise von Franz, Honorary Patron

**Studies in Jungian Psychology
by Jungian Analysts**

Daryl Sharp, General Editor

The Eden Project
In Search of
the Magical Other

JAMES HOLLIS

James Hollis is the author of four other titles in this series:
The Middle Passage: From Misery to Meaning in Midlife (1993)
Under Saturn's Shadow: The Wounding and Healing of Men (1994)
Tracking the Gods: The Place of Myth in Modern Life (1995)
Swamplands of the Soul: New Life in Dismal Places (1996)

Canadian Cataloguing in Publication Data

Hollis, James, 1940-
    The Eden project: in search of the magical other

(Studies in Jungian psychology by Jungian analysts; 79)

Includes bibliographical references and index.

ISBN 0-919123-80-5

1. Interpersonal relations. 2. Jungian psychology.
I. Title. II. Series.

BF636.H64 1998   158.2   C98-930316-0

INNER CITY BOOKS
Box 1271, Station Q, Toronto, ON M4T 2P4, Canada
Telephone (416) 927-0355 / Fax (416) 924-1814
Web site: www.inforamp.net/~icb / E-mail: icb@inforamp.net

Honorary Patron: Marie-Louise von Franz.
Publisher and General Editor: Daryl Sharp.
Senior Editor: Victoria Cowan.

INNER CITY BOOKS was founded in 1980 to promote the
understanding and practical application of the work of C.G. Jung.

Cover: "Desire," monoprint by Vicki Cowan, © 1997.

Index by Daryl Sharp.

Printed and Bound in Canada by Thistle Printing Limited

CONTENTS

See final pages for descriptions of other Inner City Books

To our children, as always:
Taryn and Tim, Jonah and Seah,
and welcome to Nicholas James.

And to my colleagues at the Philadelphia Jung Institute,
and to the good people of the
C.G. Jung Educational Center of Houston, Texas.

Preface
The Cardinal at My Window

My home office has glass walls on two and a half sides, with book-cases and paintings on the rest. For two years now, a male cardinal has appeared two to four times a day and repeatedly banged into the window. Although there are objects on the window sills that make it clear something is there, he has continued to bang away, nearly every day, these many months. By now analysands are accustomed to his noisy interjections. In fact, one day a woman who had been trying to wring a relationship out of a very frightened and passive man said, "It's like banging my head against a glass wall. I see him but he can't be reached." At that moment the cardinal served his holy office and she got the point, even laughed at herself.

Various self-appointed ornithological theorists have offered explanations for the cardinal's behavior. Some have said that he is very aggressive and seeks to attack his own kind in the reflection. Others have suggested an alternative explanation which I find resonant, whether it be true or not. They say he has lost his mate and believes he has just seen her. With unbounded joy, unquenchable fervor, he flies to her and is stunned, over and over. I had seen his mate and their brood two years previously, and see them no more, hence this theory haunts and holds me. If it is true, it is heartbreaking. He, then, is like us.

While it is clear that he has stoutly resisted behavioral modification and negative reinforcement, I still fantasize that he has the chance for consciousness, for reflection upon his enchantment by reflection. I fantasize that he does know his mate is gone forever, but continues to fling himself against that invisible wall because he still hopes, still seeks. And he will never stop.

When I was a child during World War Two a song titled "Now is the Hour" was popular. The lyrics included such memorable lines as these:

Soon you'll be sailing
Far across the sea.
While you're away,
Oh please remember me.
When you return,
You'll find me waiting here.

I had certainly been to the train station to watch the soldiers and sailors leaving, and I understood the meaning of the casualty lists in the newspaper and the gold stars in the windows. For reasons I can only report and not understand, I used to sing that song on a street corner and weep unashamedly. Only now can I conclude that I somehow knew, before full consciousness of attachment and loss, separation anxiety, yearning and the finality of bereavement, that such lines described our heartbreaking journey.

Even as I type these words, the cardinal persists in his futile opus. As do we.

Introduction

All relationships begin, and end, in separation.

Through the bloodweb of our mothers, we start out connected to the pulse and rhythm of the cosmos. And then we are torn from the Mother, separated from the cosmos, separated from the gods, separated forever. And we close all the relationships of our lives though that separation we call death. That grinning ghastly guest is even a part of the marital ceremony, reminding the couple who are just now swearing eternal devotion that, inevitably, they are also committing themselves to loss.

All too soon, one of them will leave the other—and I am not thinking here of divorce. If statistics reign, the man will die some seven years before the women. If chance reigns, she may go first. If whimsical fate intervenes in the form of a head-on collision on their way home from a neighborhood restaurant, it's anybody's guess. One way or another, both will suffer the loss of relationship. Should their plane go down with both aboard, we may say they were together, but still, in the end, each loses the other, suffers the loss of relationship, or at least that most tangible expression of it—the caring, attendant presence of one to the other.

Perhaps even more significantly, they will have spent their lives in the context of a deeper, more subtly lost relationship. They will have spent the bulk of their journey suffering the loss of relationship with their own best selves. We live our lives estranged—from others, from the gods, and worst of all from ourselves. Intuitively, we all know this. We know that we are our own worst enemies. We never stop seeking to reconnect, to find home again, and in the end we simply leave it in a different way. Perhaps there is no home to which we can return. We can't return to the womb, though we try, and few of us are confident of a future celestial home. So we live, always homeless, whether we know it or not.

In the past few years I have spent approximately two weekends a month—fall, winter and spring—giving lectures, seminars and workshops in North America and abroad. No matter what the title of the presentation, the greatest number of questions addresses the matter of relationship. Is this a sign of its importance? Surely, yes. Is this a sign of how overrated relationship is? Surely, yes. Is there something transpiring beneath the surface that requires the reframing of such ubiquitous, often urgent questions, something that puts them into a larger context? Yes, surely yes.

This book is essentially an essay on the psychodynamics of relationship. Its intention is heuristic, to provoke thought and response, and to serve as a sort of corrective to the generalized fantasies about relationships that permeate our culture. It is not meant to be a practical guide on how to fix a relationship. Rather it is an effort to evoke deeper reflection on the nature of relationship, to provide a challenge to enlarged personal responsibility in relationships, and to inspire a desire for personal growth as opposed to the fantasy of rescue through others. Its premises may be disappointing to some, and as a matter of fact I don't care much for them myself, but they are, I believe, more practical and more ethical than the many alternatives that float through our popular culture.

Throughout the text I use the terms *self* (meaning oneself) and capital-O *Other*. This is a deliberate effort to discern what is universal in relationships, as opposed to what is gender-bound, or cultural only. For this reason, the terms self and Other are just as applicable to same-sex relationships as to heterosexual.

The use of *self*—not to be confused with capital-S *Self,* Jung's term for the holistic intentionality of the human organism—is meant to refer to our conscious sense of who we are, quite apart from the fact that we can know only a tiny fragment of that huge mystery which we embody. Similarly, the word Other is capitalized as a reminder of how huge, how cosmic, another person may become in our psychic mythology. For the child, the parent as Other is as infinite as the idea of God is to the adult. The use of these terms then, is meant to be a reminder of the universal, archetypal dynamics of relationships, quite apart from the obvious fact that each relationship is unique, each influenced profoundly by the particularities of time, place, culture, family of origin and the like.

Similarly, I will from time to time use the term *marriage,* referring not to the legal formality, but to a commitment in depth made by two people of either gender or sexual predilection. A marriage vow is a guarantee of nothing certain, but it purports to be an expression of intentionality which is serious, long term and in depth. One of the implicit demands of marriage is that issues are to be faced and worked through, rather than evaded. And thus, let us not "to the marriage of true minds admit impediments."

The exploration of this theme obliges us to explore the polyfaceted character of relationships. We need to acknowledge that the character of all our relationships arises out of our first relationships, which we internalize and experience as an unconscious, phenomenological relationship to ourselves as well. Out of that relationship comes the depth, tenor and agenda of all others. Thus we will necessarily explore the origins of our sense of self, whence derives our interaction with ourselves, with others and, finally, with the Wholly Other—the transcendent.

If there is a single idea which permeates this essay it is that *the quality of all of our relationships is a direct function of our relationship to ourselves.* Since much of our relationship to ourselves operates at an unconscious level, most of the drama and dynamics of our relationships to others and to the transcendent is expressive of our own personal psychology. *The best thing we can do for our relationships with others, and with the transcendent, then, is to render our relationship to ourselves more conscious.*

This is not a narcissistic activity. In fact, it will prove to be the most loving thing we can do for the Other. The greatest gift to others is our own best selves. Thus, paradoxically, if we are to serve relationship well, we are obliged to affirm our individual journey.

1

The Lost Garden
Acquiring a Sense of Self

It is no accident that all peoples, past and present, have had their mythology of a lost Paradise. Sometimes they characterized this catastrophe as a fall from grace, a separation or a disconnection. Sometimes the cause is rumored to be the result of some human transgression, sometimes due to the capriciousness of the gods. No one ever claims to personally remember this blessed place, but the ancestors, the ancient ones, the Anasazi, remembered. They, the storied ones, were there, in the blissful Garden, but we contemporary folk always experience ourselves as outside, estranged, adrift.

Perhaps this tribal memory is but the neurological hologram of our own birth trauma, a separation from which we never fully recover. Perhaps a clue may be found in the two trees of Eden in the Genesis myth. One is the Tree of Life and the other is the Tree of Knowledge. Of the former one may eat, but eating of the latter begins the joyless trek out of Paradise. In moving from the Tree of Life, or life instinctually connected, to the Tree of Knowledge, which is the birth of civilization, the race moves from the intimate familiarity of like with like to a strickened consciousness, which can only come from the subject-object split.

Nobody remembers when consciousness began, when the first shards of sundered experience associated with other shards and became a *this* over against a *that*, a *me* over against a *you*. But from this unpredictable and uncontrollable moment derives a "sense of self," an ego so fragile it must fortify itself in provisional identities and hubris. Pretending to be Lord of the Cosmos, it trembles within the shadow memory of its painful origins. How quickly it rationalizes its thousand thousand adaptations, its long surge up and out of the primal muck. How threatened it is by the pull back and down.

15

Jung's use of the term Self, as distinguished from the ego, is meant to honor the mystery that we are. The Self, like God, is essentially unknowable. So one must speak both of the mystery of God and the mystery of the Self. The Self is not an object or even a goal, but an activity, a process. Gerard Manley Hopkins expressed it beautifully:

> Each mortal thing does one thing and the same:
> Deals out that being indoors each one dwells;
> Selves—goes itself; myself it speaks and spells,
> Crying What I do is me: for that I came.[1]

The Self is the purposiveness of the organism, the teleological intention of becoming itself as fully as it can. As the rhizome contains the fullness of the flower, so the unified self-hood of the organism is expressed through the variegations of root, stem, flower, pistil and stamen. The Self is unknowable, though its intentionality may be inferred from its expression through the venues of body, affect, cognition, symptom, dream image and the like. "Reading" the intentionality of the Self is the prime task of Jungian-oriented therapy and presumed to be the key to healing. As the Self embodies the totality of the organism and its mysterious, autonomous activity, so we may never know it fully any more than a swimmer could know the ocean, or a thinker conjugate the dome of Heaven. Hence the fragile ego must content itself with "a sense" of Self, the Self forever unknown, unknowable.

Accordingly, we are always left with partiality though we may believe we know ourselves fully. There is, in fact, no greater folly than such a hubristic claim. In Greek tragedy, one feels the earth shudder when a protagonist claims complete self-knowledge. At that moment one may be certain that the gods begin their work—to stun the person back to the proper humility of Socratic questioning. Jung said a neurosis is like an offended or neglected god, meaning that the extent to which the ego becomes too one-sided reflects how much one is denying the depth, breadth and multiplicity of the Self.

---

[1] "As Kingfishers Catch Fire," in *A Hopkins Reader*, p. 67.

Once the dream-time in the Garden is truncated, the shock of separation is so systemic, so seismic, that it remains imprinted on the neurological pathways, abiding in the unconscious as lost connectedness. It is no accident that the primary motive, the hidden agenda in any relationship, is the yearning to return. It is the cardinal's project, the Eden project, the professed aim of the Romantic poets, the yearning for the Beloved. It is essentially a religious search, as attested to by the etymology of the word "religion," from Latin *religare,* to tie back to, reconnect with.

Consciousness is achieved only through the loss of the Other, and the perception that the Other is truly Other. This is the source of the baby's cry and of Edvard Munch's famous work, *The Scream.* Watch the infant's angst as it is separated from the mother's bosom. Watch how it seeks and sucks and hopes to consume her in order to merge with her again. The care and feeding of the infant then becomes a subtle combination of 1) reassurance that the Other is there, and 2) progressive separations imposed on the child. In fact, one might say that the primary psychological task of the parent is to ease the burden but prepare the passage into full separation, into that later state we call adulthood. How this challenge is met constitutes the single largest contribution to the psychological heritage of the child. Offering reassurance while progressively "abandoning" is the paradoxical crux of parenting.

Jung compared the cost of consciousness with a Promethean burden—the illuminating fire is stolen, but at a price paid in blood. Each day takes the child a step further from the memory of the Garden. "Our birth is but a sleep and a forgetting," as Wordsworth wrote of the fading Garden.[2] Or as Dylan Thomas recalled,

> Nothing I cared, in the lamb white days, that time would take me
> Up to the swallow-thronged loft by the shadow of my hand,
> In the moon that is always rising,
> Nor that riding to sleep

---

[2] "Ode: Intimations of Immortality from Recollections of Early Childhood," in *The Norton Anthology of Poetry,* p. 552.

I should hear him fly with the high fields
And wake to the farm forever fled from the childless land.[3]

Stealing fire from the gods is a mythic metaphor for the birth of consciousness and culture, but it is also responsible for neurosis— the internal split between subject and object, self and Other. As the child uneasily carries this growing burden of consciousness, it desperately needs to learn what it can in order to reattach if possible, survive if not. It begins to "read" the world to discern its messages, what the world may teach, what it demands. This reading is phenomenological, which is to say experiential, rather than rational or cognitive in the conventional sense. The phenomenological reading of the world creates the child's sensibility, whence flow personality structure and survival strategies.

It is impossible for the parent to wholly manage the task described above, that of providing connection with the child while at the same time progressively separating. So the toddler wails when the parent goes out of sight. Even when diverted or mollified, the child still does not forget these injuries. Thrown by fate into this family or that, the child can only read the environment for clues. This reading is necessarily partial, that is, limited to that specific family, without awareness that an infinite variety of other models are possible. But from such partial views of the world huge decisions are made before there is sufficient consciousness to allow a differentiated understanding. In effect, the gods hand the child a prism through whose refracted light it must see, choose and be. That the prism is ground by the fortuities of a particular family and cultural overlay is only discerned much later in life, if at all.

How we read our ego-selves vis à vis the Other begins at birth. The child experiences bonding, or lack thereof, as an extrapolated statement about the world at large. Is it reliable, protective, or is it unpredictable, even hurtful? It is not an exaggeration to say that the entire course of one's life may derive from the phenomenological reading of such implicit messages. We know that when infants are

---

[3] "Fern Hill," ibid., p. 1181.

not held or reassured, they suffer what is called an anaclitic depression. They are more prone to mental and physiological retardation, and to life-threatening illness, than those who are emotionally nourished. Since nature brings the organism into life with the wherewithal to survive, it seems strange that the bonding experience plays such a determinant role. Yet clearly it does.

Similarly, the infant reads the world in other ways to figure out what it is saying. As early as six weeks, infants have been found to mirror their parent's face, emulating fear, depression, joy and so on. In this process, the child not only seeks its own grounding in some elemental reality, but also assumes the emotional reality of the Other, which is how one can have a depressed or anxious baby. Overall, the infant/child observes adult behavior as clues to what to expect of the world at large. For instance, as a child during World War Two, I perceived that the big folks around me were anxious. If they, with all their omnipotence, could be scared, then I could only conclude that it must be a frightening world into which I had come.

Moreover, the child observes the behavior of adults toward children and each other as a way of discerning not only how the world works, but also its implicit message. The child is not able to say, "Daddy is morose today because he was disappointed at work," or, "Mom is depressed and it is not about me." The child's thought process represents what anthropologists and psychologists call *magical thinking,* which is characteristic of so-called primitive cultures, children and any one of us in regressed states.

Magical thinking is characterized by grandiosity and paranoia. Thus the child believes its thoughts may have made mother ill or out of sorts, or that personal illness has resulted from misbehavior rather than, say, a virus. The infantile thought process lacks the capacity for subject-object dichotomies. It projects its fear and ignorance onto the world, misreads the data, and so is driven to omnipotent conclusions. Only decades later, perhaps, will that child be able to realize that he or she did not cause the problem in the family, that what mother and father were enacting had nothing to do with oneself, but created an atmosphere to which one necessarily had to adapt. By the time the child is three there is usually sufficient ego solidification to have a provisional sense of self, and by the time the child is five we feel it is strong enough to separate from family and join the company of others.[4]

In addition to this phenomenological reading of the world, which narrows and biases one's sense of self and Other, there are other experiences that have a huge impact on future relationships. As birth itself seems a kind of gigantic, systemic wound, so the exigencies of everyday life bring other wounds, the wounds of too-muchness and not-enoughness, engulfment or abandonment. The British psychiatrist D.W. Winnicott coined the expression "good enough" parent, which allows all of us to reclaim our parental histories. But it is nonetheless inevitable that the prime source of wounding to the child will be the parents. Since we are human, our less than perfect nature will necessarily impinge upon the child and leave its imprint forever. As any therapist knows, the primary area in which growth is blocked, or relationship stuck, usually becomes clear in processing these parent-child encounters which are internalized as complexes.[5]

Of course, it is impossible to escape the wounding of this world, nor is it desirable. A rather humorous example was once cited in the *Seattle Post Intelligencer,* which recounted that a couple in Leigh, England, had been denied their application to adopt a child because, tragically, they had too happy a marriage. They would not, it was concluded, be able to expose their charge to enough negative expe-

---

[4] Current data on the development of children in day-care centers indicates that they are more socialized, more developmentally stimulated, and more independent than stay-at-home children; however, they are more vulnerable emotionally if the working parent does not spend time with them when they are home. So such children make adaptations quicker and develop a sense of self which is more independent of the Other, but the old uncertainty, the pervasive angst endemic to our race, lurks not far beneath the surface.

[5] Jung was the first to demonstrate the existence of autonomous complexes; see "The Association Method," *Experimental Researches,* CW 2, and "A Review of the Complex Theory," *The Structure and Dynamics of the Psyche,* CW 8. [CW refers throughout to *The Collected Works of C.G. Jung]*

riences, which presumably would then leave him unfit for this world. In the infinite wisdom of this adoption agency, the capacity to suffer wounding and learn to adapt to it is crucial to the development of self. And so it is. We have wounds, and the clusters of energy that accompany them, because we have a life history. The deeper question is whether we have the wounds or they have us.

Such complexes, especially the parental imagos, are affectively charged images that have a unique, historically generated and discrete energy. When activated, they have the power to usurp the ego position and totally alter one's sense of reality. The parental complexes are usually the most influential because they constitute the original experience of relationship, and remain its chief paradigm. Again, because of the subjective misreading of these primal relationships, the power of the parental complexes to determine the character of subsequent relationships cannot be overstated.

There is no such thing as a wholly illogical behavior. It is always logical, that is, *psycho*-logical—if we can discern the affective state out of which it has come. It is, moreover, an observable fact that our reaction to a category of wounding can produce diametrically opposed strategies. Consider, for example, the two categories of inevitable childhood wounding, those of engulfment or abandonment. From each may flow radically different strategies. As the French proverb has it, *les extremes se touchent,* for underneath each is a common psycho-logic.

While it may seem simplistic to say that the traumas of life fall into one of two categories—the wound of too much or the wound of too little—think on wounding and see if each example does not come back to a fundamental dynamic of engulfment or of insufficiency. And from either category one may unconsciously choose a coping behavior that is diametrically opposed to the strategy "chosen" by someone else in the same situation. The tragedy of modern psychotherapy is that in most cases it is not truly psychological, that is, it does not track behavior back to its origins in the soul (which is what the word *psyche* means, after all). To correct the behavior without understanding the psychic dynamics is to remain superficial. While one might correct a behavior or alter a cognition, the wound to the soul will simply find another, perhaps more subtle, venue for its expression.

Consider, then, the wound of engulfment or overwhelment. Since the boundaries of the very young psyche are so permeable, the child is at the mercy of powerful outside forces. When Mom is depressed, for example, or Dad is angry, the boundaries of the child are invaded by their behavior and the emotionally charged atmosphere. As Jung unsparingly noted in the 1930s, "Parents should always be conscious of the fact that they themselves are the principal cause of neurosis in their children."[6] Moreover, and to make matters worse, not only are the behavior patterns of the parents profoundly influential in the psychic formation of the child, but so is everything of which they are unconscious. Jung explains,

> What usually has the strongest psychic effect on the child is the life which the parents (and the ancestors too, for we are dealing here with the age-old psychological phenomenon of original sin) have not lived.[7]

By "original sin," Jung means the neglect of soul that lies at the beginning of a family history and whose consequences ripple down through the generations. "Children are driven unconsciously," he notes, "in a direction that is intended to compensate for everything that was left unfulfilled in the lives of their parents."[8] The child's nature perceives, but without the capacity for reflection it is obliged to swallow what it perceives. Thus Jung observes,

> Children are so deeply involved in the psychological attitude of their parents that it is no wonder that most of the nervous disturbances in childhood can be traced back to a disturbed psychic atmosphere in the home.[9]

---

[6] "Introduction to Wickes's 'Analyse der Kinderseele,' " *The Development of Personality,* CW 17, par. 84.

[7] Ibid., par. 87.

[8] "Marriage As a Psychological Relationship," Ibid., par. 328.

[9] "Introduction to Wickes's 'Analyse der Kinderseele,' " *The Development of Personality,* CW 17, par. 80.

How, then, may a child react to being flooded by the environment other than to feel powerless in the face of the Other? Remember that we are tracking the etiology of relationships decades hence from these early perceptions of self and Other. The internalized template of such relationships includes as its central text that one is powerless. So, for example, abused children may grow up to marry abusers and find it virtually impossible to leave. It is not that they are in love with the abuser, rather that the depth of the programmed powerlessness is greater than the hurt of abuse. Any social worker will testify that it usually takes several incidents before the victim will leave the abuser or get a restraining order. For the first few times, victims will rationalize the abuse. The rationalization protects them not from their abusers, but from the enormity of the primal parent-child template; thus, unwittingly, they conspire against themselves to remain not only with the abuser but with the powerlessness of childhood.

If I have found myself essentially powerless against the Other, and what child has not, then how am I to comport myself in order to manage this distress? If I have routinely been invaded by abuse, verbal, emotional, sexual, or have more commonly been at the mercy of the moods and emotional vagaries of the parent, so I am inclined to identify with the Other.

This projective identification is seen in what is called "The Stockholm Syndrome," named for a group of ordinary citizens in Sweden who were kidnapped and held for many days by urban guerrillas. When they were finally liberated, they were found not only to have helped their kidnappers, they had also adopted their political views. Patty Hearst, who aligned herself in the end with her captors, the so-called Symbionese Liberation Army, is another familiar example. These kidnap victims were adults, not children, but such was their sense of powerlessness that in order to survive they identified with the views of those who had the power. Such adaptation is Survival 101. If even adults adapt in this way, what else can we then expect of children?

If I, as a child, sense my powerlessness in the presence of the ubiquitous Other and wish to survive, then my psyche will generate personality strategies based on the survival of the organism and the management of angst. I will learn to collude with powerlessness as a world-view, as a reflexive strategy or as a provisional personality.

One such strategy derived from the unconscious but controlling idea that I am powerless would be to devote my life to having power over others. In professional arenas I might simply appear ambitious, perhaps driven, and almost certainly rewarded for my productivity. But the driven person is never at peace with the soul, for the productivity is a defense against the angst of powerlessness. In the field of intimate relationships, this strategy plays out in being a controlling person or in being attracted to one easily controlled. The partners in such a relationship operate in the realm of power, not love,[10] since the psycho-logic of the powerless person is to seize as much power as possible and work life so as not to replay the deep fears felt as a child.

The reverse strategy, radically opposed, is equally observable. Since the child felt powerless in the face of the Other who was yet the source of well-being, so it learns to be pleasing, mollifying or overly responsible for the well-being of others. What is called co-dependence is one such anxiety-management strategy. If I am responsive to the needs of the Other, then, possibly, the Other might be there for me. The family of origin of many professional caregivers generates a high degree of self-identification in the child's fantasy that it is obliged to fix or heal the Other, in the hope that then the Other would be more responsive. Clearly the child cannot heal the parent, though it might sacrifice or bury its own nascent personality in the attempt. Likewise the adult: that early model of relationship becomes the template for later life, unconsciously driving one to take on the hopeless task of healing myriad wounded others.

Bruce Lackie observed many years ago that most professional caregivers described themselves as "the parentified child, the over-

---

[10] "Where love reigns, there is no will to power; and where the will to power is paramount, love is lacking." (*Two Essays,* CW 7, par. 78)

responsible member of the family, the mediator or go-between, the 'good child,' the burden bearer."[11] She or he is driven by "an overwhelming sense of responsibility to an intrapsychic symbiosis with his or her family."[12] More recently, Edward Hanna wrote that such a person, "during early childhood, accurately perceives that he or she is needed to maintain parental narcissistic equilibrium."[13]

Thus the problem of powerlessness subtly works its way through the life of the individual. One may even go so far as to choose—if that is the right word, for it is surely an unconscious choice—to have relationships only with weak or wounded persons so that the template of care-giving is served. One woman gasped the day she realized she had married her father for the second time. Her parent had been a very troubled soul, severely alcoholic. Her first husband had the same problems. So she divorced him and searched for a man who was a teetotaler. She found him and years later realized that although he did not drink, he was unable to hold a steady job, and that once again she had become the emotional and financial caretaker for the family. How deeply, unconsciously, the patterning runs, and makes our choices.

Still another pattern which may derive from the child who felt invaded or crowded is to need emotional space at all times. One man could make love with his partner, but then would have a panic attack simply when they held each other. Apparently the sexual act was less intimate, therefore less risky, than the emotional closeness of postcoital tenderness. Such persons often choose partners who themselves have difficulty with closeness, so that they may together have a de facto contract that legitimizes, even legislates, protective distance. Many therapists will recognize this common pattern in a relationship, a ballet of approach and avoidance, where one partner needs reassuring closeness and the other is more comfortable with

---

[11] "The Families of Origin of Social Workers," p. 21.
[12] Ibid.
[13] "The Relationship between the False Self Compliance and the Motivation to Become a Professional Helper," p. 46.

distance. One draws close, seeking reassurance, while the other, feeling invaded, draws back, raising the anxiety level of both. In the latter's need for protective space is the desire to do what the child could not do, that is, keep the intrusive Other at bay and preserve a fragile psychic integrity.

While any of us may experience transient moods of wishing either greater distance or closeness, these general patterns are often so deeply programmed by one's psychic history that they control the choice and character of all relationships. Then one is a prisoner of the past. And there are no prisons so confining as those of which we are unaware.

On the other hand, when the parental environment has been insufficiently nurturant, abandoning emotionally if not literally, then the child feels a desperate need for connection with the Other. Again, diametrically opposed strategies may arise. Given the magical thinking of the child, the inability to comprehend that what happens outside is Other (and not an expression of self), the child will often internalize the nurturant deficiencies of the Other as a statement about his or her own unworthiness. It is not, then, that the Other is wounded, depressed, exhausted—it is all my fault; I am unworthy of being loved, fed, cared for. "I am as I am treated," goes the psycho-logic.

Internalizing this diminished sense of self, I will subsequently spend my life hiding out, avoiding further pain. I will "choose" someone who will not be there for me. I will become stuck in what Freud called "the repetition compulsion"—so great is the program, and, paradoxically, so reassuring the confirmation that I shall not be reassured. This diminished sense of self is not unlike malnourishment of the body. Though the will may be strong, the necessary resources remain undeveloped. Thus, I cannot extend to that which I do not already know to be possible, in myself or in others.

The countervalent strategy for the insufficiently nourished child employs a desperate search for the redemption of the imago of the Other. Since the loss of the nurturant Other occasions enormous anxiety, I shall try to resolve this tension with a frenzied search for a stable, nurturant Other. In many ways, such relationships are addictive in character, as all addictions are anxiety management techniques, seeking to lower the distress of disconnection through some actual or symbolic connection. The wife who must phone her husband several times a day, the husband jealous of his wife's friends, the one who cannot bear to have the Other out of sight—all are suffering the addictive search for reassurance by trying to fix that which is forever elusive, intrinsically unfixable.

Think of William Faulkner's "A Rose for Miss Emily," wherein a woman, to prevent her lover from leaving her, poisons him and sleeps with his sweetly odiferous corpse for decades. So great is the terror of abandonment. Think of the stalker who cannot bear to be separated from the presumed Beloved. Think of the psycho-logic operating in the person who commits suicide because of the loss of a relationship: "I will kill myself lest something terrible happen to me without the Other, without whom I will surely perish anyway."

So the terrible search is launched, the search for the permanent, omnipotent Other who will heal the wound of the child. What therapist has not worked with the so-called borderline personality, whose chief features include emotional lability, transient relationships and a deep terror of abandonment? These sad souls live hellish lives, for they cannot handle the quotidian tensions of commitment, must compulsively idealize each new partner, and yet suffer the inevitable recurrence of loss. Tears and drug use are common, as is self-scarification.

One women followed her psychiatrist to the parking lot, trailed his car, staked out his home, phoned his private number, sought to seduce him in sessions, and through it all considered herself unworthy of his attention. Since she could not believe in his professional concern for her, she could only believe he cared if they had a sexual relationship, even as she knew that were their relationship to be sexualized, she would only suffer still another betrayal of her emotional integrity.

These, then, are the twin strategies for dealing with the experience or fear of abandonment by the Other—to diminish oneself and thus avoid the recurrent pain, and/or to desperately seek connection—often having "chosen" precisely an Other who would only replicate the original experience. Again, the profound power of early psychic programming looms over all.

Are we doomed to these patterns? Surely we are free to be and to behave otherwise. Yes, but that requires a high degree of conscious awareness of the pattern, and we can only know something is a pattern when we have done it several times. Moreover, until midlife or later we have seldom gained sufficient ego strength to reflect upon our choices. The young person is still too unconscious and cannot risk any self-doubt in the already shaky enterprise of life. Even aging does not necessarily produce consciousness. Think of those who have had multiple marriages, undeterred by the intimation of a pattern in the dynamics of their relationships, unaware of the unconscious templates dictating their choices as they set off in search of a new Beloved.[14]

Only when one has suffered the collapse of projections onto the Other, or tracked the symptomatology to its lair, may one begin to recognize that the enemy is within, that the Other is not what he or she may seem, and that one is summoned to a deep personal accounting before one can begin to clear the terrain for true relationship. One does not come to such recognitions easily, without having suffered failure, shame, rage or humiliation. But in such dreary states may be found the beginning of insight into oneself, without which no lasting relationship may be achieved.

The school of psychology generically known as Object Relations has influenced many other psychologies, including Jungian. Its name derives from the recognition of the crucial importance of the

---

[14] As I write these words in June of 1997, the death of an esteemed gentleman, Glynn "Scotty" Wolfe, is noted on the news. This worthy cleric had, it seems, twenty-nine legal marriages before his departure at the age of eighty-eight to a superordinate realm. He reportedly divorced one wife for eating sunflower seeds, and another for using his toothbrush. His last wife had twenty-three marriages of her own—the record holder for women. He died alone, for each refused to move to the other's estate.

"primal objects," most specifically mother and father, in the formation of one's operative personality. It is not that we do not have an inherent personality or an inherent temperament; we do, as any parent knows from their earliest observations of their children. But that inherent nature is influenced, channeled, sometimes warped, so that one becomes the creature of necessary adaptations. The price of civilization, as both Jung and Freud observed, is neurosis. Socialization is necessary, but with each adaptation one moves further from the Garden.

Elsewhere I have written at length about how one acquires a "false self" (another term coined by Winnicott).[15] I understand the false self to be an assemblage of behaviors and attitudes toward self and Other whose purpose is the management of the existential angst experienced by the child. The development of this provisional personality is inevitable since one is obliged to acquiesce to the dynamics of the family of origin and other cultural forces. With each adaptation the Garden fades, and one has a tragically distanced relationship with oneself. As Anne Sexton remembers on behalf of the child,

> The world wasn't
> yours.
> It belonged to
> the big people
> . . . . it is dark,
> where are the big people,
> when will I get there.[16]

It is no exaggeration to describe progressive self-estrangement as tragic. It is the very stuff of classical Greek tragedies, which hinge on the fact that what befalls the protagonists is a result of their having made choices from where they could not see clearly, did not sufficiently know themselves—could not see what they could not see. Out of this *hamartia,* this wounded vision of self and world,

---

[15] See *The Middle Passage: From Misery to Meaning in Midlife,* pp. 9ff.
[16] "The Fury of Overshoes," in *The Norton Introduction to Poetry,* pp. 15f.

wrong choices inevitably follow, with attendant consequences. Centuries later, we have the same experience.

Consider the obvious, then, that we can hardly have a conscious, efficacious relationship with the Other when we have a deeply wounded relationship with ourselves. Consider, then, how difficult it is to have any relationship at all. All that I do not know about myself, all of my secret projects for healing myself of the wounds derived from my culture and family of origin, I am now imposing on you. All the complexes I have acquired in my life on this earth, you will have to suffer from me. How could I do that to you, while professing to love you? How can you do that to me, while professing to love me?

Were we to survey one another's psyche, would it not be so murky at times that nothing could be seen? Or, more likely, would we not see scattered clusters of energy—complexes—which, like planets, have their own atmosphere and are forever casting penumbras over each other? And how could we speak of *love,* that great fantasy, narcotic, our reason for being ("Can't live, if living is without you . . ."), that redemptive hope which fuels our lives and popular culture? We say we love, yet we know not what it is. We say we love many things in many different ways. We borrow words from the Greeks who sought to differentiate these states of desire: *eros, caritas, philos, storgé, agape.* And yet we sense the shadowy beast behind our purest motives:

> . . . a stupid clown of the spirit's motive . . .
> stretches to embrace the very dear
> with whom I would walk without him near.[17]

Who among us can ever know ourselves well enough to be capable of *agape,* an expression of what we might oxymoronically call "disinterested love," that is, love wholly invested in the well-being of the Other, without the shadow of self-interest cruising beneath the surface like a surly shark?

---

[17] Delmore Schwartz, "The Heavy Bear Who Goes with Me," in Richard Ellmann and Robert O'Clair, eds., *Modern Poems: An Introduction to Poetry,* p. 320.

Consider the courage of those truly willing to look within and own what they find. In his autobiographical *Memories, Dreams, Reflections,* Jung tells of his self-analysis, of attending to his own depths, and repeatedly being brought up short. "Aha, here is another thing I did not know about myself." What courage it takes to pursue such repeated humbling. This is why he elsewhere observed that the most profound encounters with the Self are usually experienced as defeats for the ego, that is, repudiations of the Faustian fantasy of knowledge as a form of power.

Or consider the courage of Oedipus who had to know, though he feared that what he had to know might destroy him. His mother-lover-consort Jocasta urges him to close down the investigation. No smoking guns for her. Beyond this point lies danger. Abandon hope all ye who enter! But he has to know, and while that knowledge is destructive of the ego world he has constructed, his suffering at last brings him to Colonus where the gods bless him for his journey.

No one enters the therapist's office whose adaptive strategies are still working. One enters therapy precisely because they have failed. One finds oneself making self-defeating choices in spite of the best of motives; suffering the recurrence of primal wounds such as abandonment or overwhelment, retreating before the insurgencies of the Self whose displeasure is expressed in depression, phobias, addictions and the like. Dragged, as it were, to face oneself, one is forcibly positioned where the Self may be heard.

This encounter, which Jung called an *Auseinandersetzung,* and the Greeks called *metanoia,* brings a change of orientation through which a new sense of self may emerge. None of us who has gone through such sea-changes has ever volunteered. We were dragged there, kicking and screaming, and no doubt we will be dragged there again.

Jungians view the psyche not as a monarchy, as the ego would have it, or even as a central intelligence agency, but rather as an entity that is polyfaceted, polymorphous, polysemous, polytheistic. So there are many voices, many intimations, many directives, some heard, some not, but all persuasive. Which voice is mine? ego asks.

All of them, Self insists. But I am looking for the Zen face I had before the world was made, ego implores. And yet does Self reincarnate anew, like Krishna and his many avatars.

So we bring ourselves to relationship. With scant knowledge of ourselves, we seek our identity in the mirror of the Other, as we once did in Mom and Dad. With all the wounds of this perilous condition we seek a safe harbor in that Other who, alas, is seeking the same in us. With the thousand adaptive strategies derived from the fortuities of fated time, fated place, fated Others, we contaminate the frail present with the germs of the past. We bring the immensity of the cardinal's project, the yearning to merge with the Other, the one who will protect, nurture and save us.

2

Going Home
The Eden Project

They wanted me to tell the truth,
so I said I'd lived among them
for years, a spy,
but all that I wanted was love . . . .
I said I was emotionally bankrupt,
would turn any of them in for a kiss.
I told them how a kiss feels
when it's especially undeserved.
—Stephen Dunn, "What They Wanted."

Sometimes I forget completely
What companionship is.
Unconscious and insane, I spill sad
energy everywhere.
—Rumi, "Sometimes I Forget Completely."

Eros, Projection and the Magical Other

Eros, we are told by the Greeks, was the oldest of the gods, present in all primordial expressions of the life force, and at the same time the youngest, renewed in every moment. His name meant desire, a word which itself comes from *de sidus,* "of the star." So Eros involves yearning for the Other, whether mortal or immortal. It is goal oriented, directed toward the Other as some guiding star.

According to Hesiod, Eros arose out of Chaos. Thus, out of the primal broth came a consurgence of energy toward form, toward connection, toward creation. Still another tradition had it that Eros was born of the confluence of Aphrodite and Ares, who both knew something of desire. Eros's cultural transformation into Amor, and Cupid in Latin, is well known. The former is present, for example, in the tradition of courtly love and the Minnesingers of the Middle

33

Ages, and the latter in the cherubic archer with wounding arrows of desire. By our decadent time, he has deteriorated from some deeply energic, wounding passion to a fat little kid with draping diaper and toylike bow and arrow, best fit for greeting cards and graffiti. Well, all good things can become demonic when one-sided, unbalanced by their opposite. Cupid becomes cupidity, the excess of desire. Such has been the fate of most classical gods, which is why Jung characterized neuroses as gods who had been wounded.

Eros has often been further narrowed in our time to the merely erotic. Defined elementally, eros is the desire for connection. Surely sexuality may be subsumed under that motive, but eros is richly differentiated and may be found in many venues. As he is a god, divine Eros is always present, at least implicitly, when connection is sought, though the god himself may be forgotten, ignored, violated, trivialized or, paradoxically, adored. Music is erotic; prayer is erotic; violence is erotic; language is erotic . . . the permutations are infinite because the gods are infinite.

To designate such diverse human activities as "erotic" may seem strange, even as the invocation of a deity may seen strange to the modern sensibility. But the ancients had it right—wherever there is depth, there is also the divine. Where the gods are is where meaning may be experienced. What the gods most ask of us is that we attend them, that is, bear conscious witness to their energies, of which their forms are but the material husk. If we do not serve that depth energy which a god represents in whatever erotic act, then we have violated something profound.[18]

Eros is dynamic and shape-shifting. As energy, it is always going somewhere, seeking to connect, to fill in, to transcend. Just as Nature, we are told, abhors a vacuum, so our psyche is terrified by emptiness. Seeking to fill that emptiness, we all too often fill it with ourselves. Wheresoever space opens, into that hole flies projection.

---

[18] How we remember and trace the movement of these veiled energies, the track of these invisible ones, is the subject of my book, *Tracking the Gods: The Place of Myth in Modern Life.*

Projection, as a psychological phenomenon, is ubiquitous and inevitable. Psychic energy is, to borrow Freud's phrase, polymorphously perverse; that is, it is forever taking, twisting, turning and recreating in order to fill the lacunae. It employs multiple strategies, of which splitting, substituting and sublimating are but a few. Eros splits into polarities, hence love and hate may be present in any given relationship. Eros substitutes as it seeks the Cosmic Other in the frail vessel of the Beloved. Eros sublimates as it transfers its cosmic need to the vacant skies in search of the Great Father or Eternal Mother. Just as a tiny square of celluloid can project prehistoric monsters onto a distant screen, so the rush of eros energy can, filtered by the idiosyncratic history of the individual, fill even the heavens with its psychic portrait.

All projection occurs unconsciously, of course, for the moment one observes, "I have made a projection," one is already in the process of taking it back. More commonly, we only begin to reclaim our purchase on consciousness when the Other fails to catch, hold, reflect our projection. If there is a central law of the psyche, it is that what is unconscious will be projected. This is why Jung observed that "when an inner situation is not made conscious, it happens outside, as fate."[19] But since the psyche consists of a multitude of split-off shards of energy, complexes and archetypal forms (to which Jung granted near-mythological status with names like *anima, animus, shadow),* virtually all of which are unconscious, there is always ample opportunity for projection. As I can never know the unconscious, by definition or practice, so I can never know what energies may be acting autonomously and casting a veil of Maya, or illusion, over the world as I know it.

Kant cautioned two centuries ago that one can never know the *Ding-an-Sich,* the "thing-in-itself," that is, never know the essential character of external reality, but only the subjective, phenomenological workings of one's own psychic experience. In tautological terms, we may only experience our experience! In his insistence on

---

[19] *Aion,* CW 9ii, par. 126.

the radical subjectivity of human experience, Kant ended meta-physics, the search for absolute reality, but thereby made necessary psychology, the tracking of interior process.

"All relationships, *all* relationships, begin in projection." With this simple, categorical statement I began a workshop two years ago in a West coast city. I had not finished the rest of the paragraph before that first sentence was seized upon by two separate persons who took vocal and emotional exception. "But sometimes you just know," each insisted. "You know this is the right one." Only the presence of an invisible complex, like a mine toward which the ship hurries, could account for so much urgent energy. Each insisted that the Other could be known in an instant, especially that Other whom we would consider the Beloved. Of course we all do have an intui-tive function, which some of us rely on more than do others, and sometimes to good effect. We "sense" something to be true; we "smell" a rat; we feel "in our bones." But we are also often wrong.

I resisted asking the questioners if they were still with their Be-loved, the one they knew was "right" from that first moment. I wondered if that great initial insight had proved true over the years, whether the relationship with the Other had had genuine staying power. Was the eros connection as strong today as in that first mo-ment? I suspected not, for it seldom is. But such is the power of an idea, an affectively charged idea whose proper definition is a com-plex. To call an idea like this a complex is in no way to derogate it; a complex is, simply said, an idea with a lot of energy that knocks about autonomously in our psychic cellar.

The power of a complex cannot be overemphasized; indeed, it is what drives both individual history and collective culture. In par-ticular, two great ideas, or complexes, animate the lives of us all. Both are false, and we consciously know them to be so, but we find infinite ways to deny, dissimulate, rationalize.

The first great false idea is the fantasy of immortality. We know we are mortal; we have a good grasp of the statistics; we read the newspaper. Yet there is a place in each of us that is quick to con-sider ourselves exempt. Surely we are exceptions, somehow, and will live forever. Of course we know otherwise, but the fantasy has enormous durability.

The other great false idea that drives humankind is the fantasy of the Magical Other, the notion that there is one person out there who is right for us, will make our lives work, a soul-mate who will repair the ravages of our personal history; one who will be there for us, who will read our minds, know what we want and meet those deepest needs; a good parent who will protect us from suffering and, if we are lucky, spare us the perilous journey of individuation. Virtually all popular culture is fueled by this idea and its fallout—the search for the Magical Other, finding him or her, the dismaying discovery of this Other's humanness, and the renewed search. . . . Listen to the next ten songs on the car radio. Nine of them will be about the hunt for the Magical Other.[20]

Behind the search for the Magical Other lies the archetypal power of the parental imagos. Our first experience of ourselves is in relationship to these Primal Others, usually mother or father. Consciousness itself arises out of that splitting of the primal *participation mystique* which characterizes the infant's sensibility. The paradigms for self, for Other, and the transactions between, are formed from these earliest experiences. They are hard-wired into our neurological and emotional network.

It has been noted that couples who live together for a long time often come to resemble each other. (People and their dogs can begin to look alike too, but that is another story). Or, as one enters the fifties, one's partner may seem to resemble one's parent. Think of those older folks who address or refer to each other as Ma and Pa, Mom and Dad, Mother and Father. Such phenomena suggest that the original attraction to the partner was in great part guided by the parental imago. That unconscious image is projected onto potential partners until someone comes along who can catch and hold it.

One cannot know the depth and power of such an imago pre-

---

[20] Would it be stretching to see this search echoed in the longing for the perfect car, job, house or whatever? Yes, possibly, but on the other hand, maybe not.

cisely because it is unconscious, and because it was programmed before consciousness was there to reflect upon it. Sometimes one will be aware of a certain quality that derives from the field of conscious relationship with the parent. The partner sought must be steady and trustworthy, for example, or offer the sense of security a parent once did. More often, the pathology of the parent-child relationship is calling the shots. How many abused children have formed relationships with abusers, helplessly replicating the primal paradigm? How many adult children of alcoholics find addictive personalities with whom to bond? Often these patterns slumber in the unconscious and do not emerge for decades. Sometimes a person ends a relationship and consciously seeks a quite different person with whom to bond, only to repeat the familiar dynamics that characterized the previous relationship.

What is repetitive, of course, is the psychodynamic of the relationship, not its outer appearance. Who in their right mind would seek out someone and say, "I want you to repeat my childhood wounding. I will love you because you are so familiar." But we do this all the time. It is truly frightening to realize how little one is conscious in the formation of intimate relationship, how powerful is our programmed desire for what we have known. What is known is what is sought, even if what is known is wounding.

So it is that the Magical Other is loaded up with all the detritus of our psychic history. If there is an enemy that owns us, it is the power of that history, with its ability to usurp consciousness, warp perspective, contaminate choice, and seek its own replication. Among the several tasks of psychotherapy is the confrontation with such history, at least as much as may be brought to consciousness through the examination of behavior patterns, symptomatology and dreams. This encounter is sometimes shocking, occasionally depressing and always humbling. Just as the mature adult may look back on the choices of adolescence with pained recognition of how little one understood, so too the unconscious dynamics which drove one toward a certain kind of relationship may one day come to the surface. And what we then see is seldom a pretty picture.

This Crazy Thing Called Love

As one reads these sentences, agreeing here, disagreeing there, but generally in accord with the flow of reason, the heart suddenly proclaims: "But what about love?"

Ah yes, that wonderful thing, love, that magic elixir without which we perish. And what, we ask, is this love? Is it properly defined in the rather cynical words attributed to the poet John Ciardi, "Love is the word used to label the sexual excitement of the young, the habituation of the middle-aged, and the mutual dependence of the old"? Or is it the magical force which makes the world go round, makes the world brand new (as the Greeks observed with Eros), or makes us miserable without it? Could one even agree on a universal definition? Does not its strange power smack of magic? Does it not dissemble and reappear as that energy which fires the imago of the Beloved? Perhaps we need to back off a bit and ease our way into this love business.

Surely the fundament of love is the flow of energy, whether unidirectional or reciprocal. So we may say we love our pets, love our country, love Monet, love baked brie, apple pie or golf. We certainly invest energy along the way in friendship. The younger one is, the more transient those friendships seem, for they are fragile and ill-withstand the test of conflict or disappointment.

Some years ago, in an article in *Psychology Today,* Paul Wright of the University of North Dakota summed up his research findings on love and friendship as follows:

> Love relationships differ from friendships in four areas. Love relationships are more exclusive, more intense in emotional expression, and more permanent than friendships, and are viewed as more dominated by social rules and expectations.[21]

Other researchers in that article identified the following eight characteristics as common to both love relationships and friendship: enjoyment of the other, mutual assistance, respect, spontaneity, ac-

---

[21] Keith E. Davis, "Near and Dear: Friendship and Love Compared."

ceptance, trust, understanding and confidence.

We may love our friends, but intimate love, it seems, carries a far higher charge. Intimacy often includes fascination with the Other, desire for exclusivity and, of course, sexual desire. Each of these characteristics suggests that intimate love relationships are far more loaded with psychic investment. Fascination derives from the Latin *fascinare,* which means "to charm." Charm in this sense is not what you learn by going to a finishing school; it means to possess, to usurp consciousness.

So, to be fascinated by the Other is to be possessed by an affective idea. This is what happens in projection. In the most rabid stage of being in love—and rabid is by no means too strong a word—one is unable to do other than obsess on the Other. One is caught in a projective identification with the heart's desire, the boundaries between self and Other dissolving again, as they did for the infant. This is the unconscious underpinning of the fascination with the Other: the search to recover the lost paradise of childhood, the original *participation mystique* with the primary caregivers.

Similarly, the demand for exclusivity in relationship clearly has its roots in the infant's total dependence on the stability of the Other. Yet a common belief in popular culture is that jealousy is a measure of how much one is loved, rather than an index of the jealous person's insecurity. "I know my partner loves me because he can't stand to see me talking with someone else." I have even heard it said, by a physically abused spouse, that the abuse was really a sign of how deeply the abuser cared.

One man I saw briefly had been married several times. He had abused and controlled all of his partners, so fragile was his sense of psychological grounding. Of course he could not sustain therapy, for the introspection involved requires a strength of character and emotional resilience he did not have. The need to keep the other solely for oneself, and here I do not mean sexual fidelity, will ultimately bear bitter fruit, as respect for the freedom of the Other is supplanted by power and the concomitant need for control.

Of sexual desire in intimate relationships we shall speak later.

But to the foregoing list differentiating intimate love from friendship, one might add two other characteristics. In an intimate relationship, one is more willing to champion the cause of the Other, for one is more deeply invested in the Other's well-being. And one is more likely to offer up personal sacrifice for the Beloved than for a friend. Many of the great love stories, of course, have such sacrifice as their cornerstone; they continue to touch us because they illustrate the human capacity to sublimate one's profound instinct for survival on behalf of a beloved Other.

In addition, we are further obliged to differentiate that formal, historic agreement we call marriage from the energy which we are calling love. By "marriage" here, I am again speaking less of the legal definition of such relationship than the depth and character of commitment which makes its dissolution less casual. It is the moral opacity of the so-called Moral Majority, as well as most governments, that leads to prohibiting same-sex marriage even as they espouse the virtues of commitment, family values and permanence.

What their bigotry offers instead is not only discriminatory, it also undermines the fundamental premise of committed relationships. As one gay man said to me recently, "I am tired of supporting heterosexual fornication with my taxes." Or as another gay man said to me, only slightly joking, "I believe in gay marriages because I believe in gay divorces." He was referring to the hope that his legal marital rights could be extended to him, not only those involving insurance, tax credits, etc., but also those rights due to each partner on the occasion of marital break-up. (In the end, for all its moralizing, the Moral Majority is neither moral nor the majority.)

Historically, love and marriage have not been synonymous; contrary to that old song, they have seldom gone together "like a horse and carriage." As a matter of fact, only in the last century and a quarter has the vox populi claimed marriage and love as one and the same. This is not to say that happily committed people have not loved each other, but rather that for most of human history the purpose of marriage was to bring stability to the culture rather than make the individual happy or serve the task of mutual individuation. Possibly the greatest number of history's marriages would, by today's standards, be described as loveless, for they were contracted arrangements made to produce, protect and nurture the young, thus to preserve the tribe, to transmit social and religious values, and to channel anarchic libido in socially useful directions.

Similarly, in many marriages love, whatever love may prove to be, is simply not the determinative value. What more commonly has brought people together, the energy which seeks synergy, are the operative complexes of each. One or both may seek to find the good parent in the other, may even wish to find an abuser in order to confirm a wounded sense of self, or may be seeking what was missing in the family of origin. Or, one may marry for a sense of transferred power.

I recall seeing two women, one of whom had referred the other. Each had the identical complaint, that their husbands were only capable of talking about business. Each woman had two decades earlier married for "love," and that quickly played out. Then each woman married a man who was several years older, affluent, "successful" and apparently a more mature choice. But each woman had transferred her own undeveloped animus onto that second husband. They had their fine houses and their expensive cars, but found they had no real relationship. Precisely those "male" qualities that had attracted them to their husbands were not only undeveloped in themselves, but had narrowed their husband's personalities, leaving them with little in common but their affluence, which brought neither happiness nor meaningful relationship.

We are reminded by ancient counsel that we should beware of getting what we want. Depth psychology echoes this: we could be getting simply what the complex wants, what the unconscious history wants, what the unlived life wants. And then, given this unholy origin, the relationship can only play out the tragic script to which it is covertly bound.

Everything, everything, seems to ride on this thing called love. We love nature, we make love, we fall into and out of it, we pursue love and ask it to save us. Romantic love, by which we mean that élan, that heightened ardor, that intense yearning for the Beloved, that frantic grappling, that profound sorrow when the Beloved is lost, that anxious uncertainty about the fixity of the Other—all this and more is both the greatest source of energy and the chief narcotic of our time. Given the erosion of the tribal myths which once helped connect our ancestors to the gods, to nature, to the tribe and to themselves, romantic love may prove to be the primary region of existential hunger in our century. One may even suggest that romantic love has replaced institutional religion as the greatest motive power and influence in our lives.

So, the search for love has replaced the search for God. Shocking thought? Untrue? Again, simply surf the stations on the radio. Almost all the popular songs express the "religiosity" of romantic love. Recall the etymology of the word religion—"to bind back to, reconnect with." Hitherto we sought this in relationship with a supreme being; now we seek it through immersion in an Other. Any given song will track the search for this Other: knowing he or she is just around the next emotional corner, the joy of finding the Right One, the confusion when the complexes make their unwanted appearance, the anger and bitterness of conflict and hurt, the anguish of loss, then back to the beginning, the renewed search—which will be found in the song on the adjacent kilocycle.

If one were to write a song which encompassed all these stages of the search for the Magical Other, one would not only make a lot of money but would be describing the chief religion of Western civilization. This romantic fantasy has even more power to move a person than its close rival, economics. Mixing T.S. Eliot and Albert Camus, one might say of the modern world, "They made money and they fornicated." Neither metaphysic worked for them for very long, but both remained unshakable goals.

The greatest power of false gods lies not in their powers of subtle seduction, but in their capacity still to command belief, unquestioning belief, even after many betrayals. Many popular songs in fact *celebrate* the heart's fierce determination to begin anew the quest for the Magical Other. The popularity of the book and film

The Bridges of Madison County testifies to the power of this religion of romance, this never-ending search. Someday, in the midst of
your humdrum life, the fated, fabulous stranger will drive into your
life, grant you transcendence and then go off forever, leaving you to
the ordinary, but soul afire. Kisses as *Kismet.* No partner, no matter
how worthy, can compete with that fantasy.

There are other ways in which love and marriage are not synonymous. Many marriages simply evolve beyond the implicit terms
of the invisible contract. Whatever complexes or programmed ideas
of self and Other may have inspired the marriage, the psyche has
moved to another place. It is not so much that people fall out of
love, but that the original controlling ideas have waned in favor of
others—or the complex has decided that the Other cannot meet the
expectations of the original agenda.

If one has not in fact grown in the course of a marriage, it has
been a dreadful disaster. Mere longevity in a marriage is not necessarily something to celebrate, for what happened to the souls of
those individuals along the way? One is reminded of the poem by
Christian Morgenstern, "The Two Asses":

> An ass in a depressive state
> Spoke thus once to his wedded mate:
>
> "I am so dumb, you are so dumb,
> Let's go and die together, come!"
>
> But as it happens almost daily,
> The two continued living gaily.[22]

I take "gaily" here to be ironic, the public face that hides a thousand cuts. For how many couples grow in roughly the same direction at roughly the same pace? Seldom do both perceive life at the
same level of consciousness or possess equal capacity to process
difficult matters. More often, one partner has outgrown the unconscious premises of the relationship while the other clings to the

---

[22] In Angel Flores, ed., *An Anthology of German Poetry from Hölderlin to Rilke,* p.
305.

original implicit bargain. The former feels frustrated, depressed; the latter feels anxious and controlling. My experience has been that most often it is the woman who seeks change and growth. Perhaps this is true, if it is, because women seem to monitor a relationship more carefully, while men seem to equate their well-being with outer parameters, such as career or possessions. They may be equally unhappy, but they are likely to differ on what to address. Women seek to recontextualize the relationship; men are more concerned to fix what is broken. Their goals are similar, but the means are poles apart.

As no popular culture has built itself upon the idea of romance more than twentieth-century America has, so none has founded itself on more shifting ground. A necessary corollary, then, is that no culture has more set itself up for disappointment than the one which seeks its affirmation in projection, illusion and delusion.

So we come back to the idea of projection. What we do not know about ourselves—and we cannot, ever, know much at all—will be projected onto the outer world.

The search for the Magical Other is evoked by the Persian poet Rumi in a poem that begins:

> The moment I heard my first love story,
> I started looking for you . . .[23]

Is not this precisely what we seek, the fated meeting with that One whom the gods have provided us, the One who will complete us, make us whole? Did not Plato, in the dialogue on love called *The Symposium,* put precisely this hope in Aristophanes's comic description of our original wholeness, our sundering by the gods for our misdeeds, and the world thereafter filled with part-souls frenetically seeking their other half? But Rumi knows better:

> . . . not knowing how blind that was.
> Lovers don't finally meet somewhere.
> They're in each other all along.[24]

---

[23] See Sam Kean and Anne Valley-Fox, *Your Mythic Journey,* p. 26.
[24] Ibid.

I have a copy of a highly sentimental nineteenth-century pre-Raphaelite painting of that magic moment when Dante espied Beatrice (Beatricca Portinari) walking by the Arno River in Florence. Dante stands to the left, stricken, his hand at his wounded breast. Beatrice comes toward him, holding a rose, suggesting not only her beauty but also hinting at the beatific vision which he later encounters in the *Paradiso*. To one side of Beatrice stands a friend dressed in blue, the medieval iconographic color of the virginal, the spiritual; on the other side is a friend garbed in red, the color of carnality and passion. It's all there. Later, this woman, whom he never knew personally, becomes Dante's soul guide, his psychopomp, who leads him up out of the Inferno toward the Divine.

Pretty powerful stuff—and all projection. What is real here is Dante's experience; what is not real is that Beatrice herself is the source of the energy that fuels his creativity and leads him to become the mythopoeic voice of his age. And it is ever thus: the one who inspires us, the Beloved, has been in us all along. Indeed, this is one of the wonderful things about projection: it spurs the release of energies that might otherwise lie dormant. This, I know, is as true of you and me as of any Dante, any artist, any entrepreneur, any auto mechanic, any waitress—anyone.

The Inner Dynamic of Projection

Our psychological history, the dynamic character of complexes forever seeking analogues ("When have I been here before?"), and the mechanism of projection all ensure that transference and countertransference dynamics are present in every relationship.

In formal analysis, one brings to each session not only the desire for consciousness, but also a carpetbag of psychological history that is dynamic, intentional and autonomous. The analyst is not free of history either, but by virtue of a long-term analysis has a good idea of what complexes might be activated by the setting and the material the analysand brings. It is not that analysis renders one fully conscious of such psychic reflexes, but rather that it better enables one to recognize their presence when they do emerge.

The following diagram applies to all relationships,[25] though intimacy usually evokes more of the primal imagos of self and Other, and the various strategies of relatedness, as well as the largest healing hopes. Again, recall that such primal imagos are largely derived from the fortuities of the parent-child relationship.

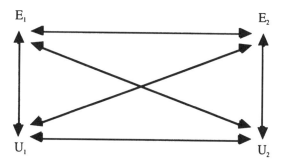

E_1 refers to the ego, or conscious sense of self, of the first party, and E_2 refers to the conscious sense of self of the Other. E represents the one we bring consciously to the table, who we think we are. U_1 is the dynamic psychological history of the first party and U_2 is the dynamic psychological history of the Other. Both terms, "dynamic" and "psychological history," are critical here. The first implies that our psychic energies are operative at all times, with an autonomy outside of ego control (just try to order up a certain kind of dream when you sleep tonight). Such dynamics are designed to protect the organism and/or further its development, and may serve either or both at any given time. Psychological history includes not only the sum of what has happened to us since birth, especially in the field of relationship, but how that has been internalized into an idiosyncratic view of the world that forms "provisional understandings" based on the premises of personal history, most of which are unconscious.

According to the diagram, there are twelve directions in which energy may travel, only two of which are conscious, with two more

[25] Adapted from Jung's schema in "The Psychology of the Transference," *The Practice of Psychotherapy,* CW 16, par. 422.

that may become conscious. The energy can flow from E_1 to E_2 (ego to ego) in either direction. It may also flow in either direction from E_1 to U_1 and E_2 to U_2. Further, when the U (dynamic psychological history) of either party is engaged—and it always is to greater or lesser degree—its contents will be projected onto the E of the Other, represented here by the two diagonal lines.[26]

When we remember the central law of projection, that what is unconscious will be either repressed or projected, it is clear that a tremendous amount of traffic transpires in any given instant of relationship. We can even observe a difference between big projections and small projections. The latter have to do with relating to the Other in programmed, habitual ways, which comes from the whole history of relationships. And the former, "big" projections, have to do with the transference of the "going home" project onto the Other—the fantasy that through him or her I will be healed, nurtured, protected and spared the awful rigors of growing up.

It is inevitable that projections occur, that transference and countertransference occur, that we have a large project in mind for the Other, for we are never courageous or conscious enough to pull it all back. We remain human in our deep longing for that suprahuman Other. The only question is to what degree we realize this.

When E_1 directs energy toward E_2, we have a conscious relationship. Two persons on a flight from Chicago to New York, or a train from Santa Fe to Houston, may converse with great animation, then separate and never think of each other again. Generally such meetings are confined to the conscious level of exchange. However, two psychic histories are present nonetheless, and one or other, or both, may be activated. Perhaps one of them has the mannerisms of a de-

---

[26] In classical Jungian thought the two U's are often referred to as anima and animus, the so-called internal feminine principle in men and internal masculine principle in women, respectively. Today such terms are undergoing major deconstruction, and possibly reconstruction. In any case, here I consider the U's as the whole field of unconscious psychological history, not only because they similarly apply in same-sex relationships, but because the unconscious material which the U encompasses includes far more than what Jung intended by anima and animus.

parted parent, or the lineaments of a loved or feared teacher. Then the unconscious is up and running, evoking the dynamics of transference or countertransference in a particular way. One could feel a strong dis-ease, or alternatively a strong attraction. How many romances, even marriages, have begun in such circumstances?

In relationships so inherently transient, a lifetime may be reenacted. We may project our imago of the beloved Other, and/or receive such a projection; or we may project our fears and hates onto others, as may they onto us. In such cases, we are transiently psychotic, in the sense that consciousness has been usurped by the contents of the unconscious. The lens of past experience passes over one's eyes, distorting our perception and creating a whole new world of choice and consequence.

What is popularly called falling in love is just such a transient psychosis. This is why such phrases as "love is blind" or *folie à deux* have been used to describe it. Look, Cupid is depicted wearing a blindfold. What good choices might arise out of blindness? In adolescence, one may be transported to the heights and depths of such madness once or twice a week. Fortunately this psychosis is usually temporary. But those moments of madness can wreak havoc on self and others—deep depression, stalking, homicide and suicide. Indeed, the day I write these lines, the quiet community of Pearl, Mississippi, is rocked by the multiple murder of school children by a teenager suffering from unrequited love.

The most popular book at the end of the eighteenth century was Goethe's *The Sorrows of Young Werther,* wherein two thwarted lovers take their lives. For several decades following, jilted or frustrated lovers were fished from the Rhein or the Neckar, or found at the bottom of some cliff, with a copy of that novel in their pocket.

Suicide is a "logical" extension of the original unconscious premise: "My soul, my reality, is in the hands of that Other." When the Other is not there for me, or spurns me, or I feel blocked by extraneous forces, I suffer a loss of the sense of self. Without a sense of self I am miserable and, so the logic goes, I shall kill myself lest I lose myself. The circular character of this argument is lost to the person in extremis. This tortuous madness is not only the subject of much popular culture, but, indeed, is earnestly sought by lovers. Such ecstasy, such transport, such transcendence, such yearning to go home again! Who does not hunger, with Faust, for example, for such a transcendent encounter with life? Who would not wish to say, with Hölderlin, that, having had such transcendence, "Once I / lived like the gods, and no more is needed."[27] Or who would not wish to cast one's lot with Rumi:

> I would love to kiss you.
> The price of kissing is your life.
>
> Now my loving is running toward my life shouting,
> What a bargain, let's buy it.[28]

The temporary payoff of other addictions—drugs, gambling, food—pales in comparison with what the transcendent Other may offer. It is not just relief from this world's pain, an anodyne to boredom and depression, but a recovery of that fabled Eden one seeks in the neurological labyrinth of our history. Nothing has greater power over our lives than the hint, the promise, the intimation, of the recovery of Eden through that Magical Other. No wonder, then, the dismay, the horror, of losing Eden again, when its precincts were glimpsed from afar. Who would want to live on, having lost it yet again? The repeated loss of Eden is the human condition, even as the hope for its recovery is our chief fantasy.

Yet, we all know that the Other, a simple, flawed human being just like ourselves, can never carry the full weight of our Eden project. Nor can we carry the Other's. Those two diagonal vectors in the relational diagram are the most active of all the twelve possibilities. Invariably, as they carry so much weighted history, so much longing, such a large hope, they will collapse. At that moment, one falls out of love, as the culture has it. More than half of all popular songs mourn this loss of the beloved Other. "Who are

---

[27] "To the Fates," in Flores, ed., *An Anthology of German Poetry*, p. 7.
[28] "Two Poems by Rumi," in R. Bly, ed., *The Soul Is Here for Its Own Joy*, p. 139.

you," "I don't know you anymore," "You've changed," "You've broken my heart"—that is, failed my Eden project. But since my Eden project, my desire to go home through you, is essentially unconscious, I am unaware of its origin in myself and can only blame you for this great disappointment.

Withdrawing Projections

In *Projection and Re-Collection in Jungian Psychology,* Zurich analyst Marie-Louise von Franz has delineated the fivefold process of projecting and then re-collecting our psychic fragments.

First, a person is convinced that his or her inner experience is truly outer, for it is experienced "out there." Thus one may fall deeply in love or deeply into suspicion. One man I knew followed his wife everywhere because he was convinced she was having affairs. He hired detectives, obliged her to take two polygraph tests, and still could not believe her protestations of fidelity. As an eight year old he had seen his mother drive away with another man and he never saw her again. He could not believe that this second woman, to whom he had given his heart, could be any different.

Or consider the projective system within which the sociopath lives. Having been deeply wounded in childhood, such a person projects the betrayal of the Primal Other onto humanity and can form no relationship without remaining in control. Losing control of the Other, the sociopath turns to violence in an unconscious repetition of the powerless of childhood. Abuse of the partner is a projective transference of the past onto the present—a dreary and wounding repetitive cycle.

The second stage of the projective process arises out of the often gradual perception of discrepancy, the widening gulf between who the Other is supposed to be and our concrete experience. Why does she act in such apparent disregard for my agenda? Why does he not seem devoted only to me? Why is she sometimes fractious and intractable? Niggling questions grow into large doubts. Doubts lead to consternation. One begins to question the reality of the Other, after all. This is troubling and accounts for the fact that so many couples move from naive relatedness to the joustings of power. If you do not act as I wish, I shall bring about your compliance by my actions. I will control you, criticize you, abuse you, withdraw from you, sabotage you. Seldom are these attitudes and behaviors conscious, but they are there, filling in the gaps.

The loss of a projection is often painful, and the broader the projection, the deeper the hurt. One has been counting on the Other to make the journey back home possible. It is the frustration of the cardinal who keeps hitting the glass and bouncing back. It is the stunned amazement of that goldfinch in James Thurber's story, "The Glass in the Field," where the bird tells his comrades, "I was flying across a meadow when all of a sudden the air crystallized on me." Often by the time a couple seeks therapy, each feels viscerally wounded by the Other. The bloodletting has been considerable. Each sees the therapist not as a neutral third party, but as a judge who will rule his or her position just. By this time, the couple has usually fallen out of love and the power principle prevails.

The third stage of the projective process, whether in or out of therapy, obliges the assessment of this new perception of the Other. One's partner must now be seen anew. What is going on between us? Who, really, *is* he/she?

The fourth stage leads one to recognize that what one perceived was actually not real, that one was not experiencing the Other out there, but the Other in here. This step represents an act of ethical courage, for it helps to lift the cosmic project off the shoulders of the Other.

The fifth stage requires the search for the origin of that projected energy within oneself. This is to ask for the meaning of the projection. Which part of me was projected, and to what end? Since projections are by definition originally unconscious, we can only withdraw them when we have sustained the suffering of discrepancy.

Apart from the pain of such discrepancies, we may detect projections in the same three ways in which we detect complexes.

Firstly, there are predictable situations in which complexes, or projections, are likely to be activated. Most generally, the entire sphere of intimacy is one such charged field in which projections are being exchanged at all times. This fact may seem depressing—it is in any case humbling—for one does not really know the Other, ever, and what we do not know we are prone to fill with our own projected material. Even those who have lived together for decades barely know each other, psychologically speaking, though they may be greatly habituated to each other.

Secondly, we may experience projection in a physical way. A churning stomach, a quickening heart, sweaty palms and so on are somatic states that can alert us to the likelihood of projection.

Thirdly, in projection the quantity of energy discharged is always disproportionate to the situation. Since the field of intimate relationship carries the burden of the "going home" project, so the largeness of energy we feel in such a relationship is evidence of the largeness of the agenda projected. This is not to say that relationships are not profoundly important, but rather that we may make them too important. Again, this is why one is bereft at the loss of the Other, sometimes suicidal, for the fantasy of recovering the lost Primal Other has crumbled. We are meant to grieve loss, of course, but too often the overvaluation of the Other is achieved only through the devaluation of oneself.

Jung reminds us of the ubiquity of projection: "The general psychological reason for projection is always an activated unconscious that seeks expression."[29] And elsewhere:

> Strictly speaking, projection is never made; it happens, it is simply there. In the darkness of anything external to me I find, without recognizing it as such, an interior or psychic life that is my own. . . . Such projections repeat themselves whenever man tries to explore an empty darkness and involuntarily fills it with living form.[30]

Having suffered the discrepancy, the loss of the Other as projected, we are left with the humbling task of becoming conscious. What we do not know can and does hurt us, and others too. Ulti-

---

[29] "The Tavistock Lectures," *The Symbolic Life,* CW 18, par. 352.
[30] *Psychology and Alchemy,* CW 12, par. 346.

mately this constitutes a moral imperative. As von Franz insists,

> We average human beings . . . will hardly be able to avoid the ne-
> cessity, for the rest of our lives, of again and again recognizing pro-
> jections for what they are, or at least as mistaken judgments. It
> seems to me, therefore, to be extremely important to bear constantly
> in mind, at the very least, the possibility of projection. This would
> lead to much greater modesty on the part of our ego-consciousness
> and to a readiness to test our views and feelings thoughtfully and not
> to waste our psychic energy in pursuing illusionary goals.[31]

Her last comment bears repeating, lest we "waste our psychic
energy in pursuing illusory goals." The mythic effort to recover the
paradisiacal Garden is profoundly human, but the more one pursues
it, the more it recedes. So it must have been for Coronado's weary
conquistadors as they urgently topped one more New Mexican hill
to see still another city of gold on the next horizon, a city which
would be gone by the time they arrived.

We must imagine a deep unconscious-to-unconscious flow of
energy between two persons, as illustrated by the bottom line in the
relationship diagram on page 47. Until they concretize the experience and find its origin, they cannot recognize that there is some
sort of *participation mystique* occurring between U_1 and U_2. A projective identification may occur in which one personality is subsumed into the other and the lines between them blurred. Could that
be how a Hitler, say, becomes the embodiment of a collective will?
Did his unconscious engage the unconscious of the fervent masses,
beyond even the projection of a hero or savior complex? It is at
least as plausible to think so as to try to explain his capacity to mobilize, absorb and direct the energies of millions through the sum of
economic and political factors.

There is little doubt that such projective identifications occur.
They feel wonderful when one senses that one has come home
through the agency of the Other; they feel diabolical if one feels

---

[31] *Projection and Re-Collection in Jungian Psychology: Reflections of the Soul,* p.
199.

possessed by the Other. How many pogroms, martyrdoms, burnings, mass hysterias have scarred history, destroyed lives, because of unconscious contamination between U_1 and U_2?

What remains in the relationship diagram is most critical of all: the vertical axes, the relationship of each party to his or her own unconscious. The quality and character of all relationships stem from this axis, yet it is the one most ignored. Again, we cannot know that of which we are unconscious, but we must never forget that the unconscious is active and projecting.

Since the content of every projection is some aspect of ourselves, what we are "seeing" in the Other is something of ourselves. It may seem ludicrous, but in this sense, what we fall in love with is some aspect of ourselves as reflected back to us from the Other. In the course of an ordinary lifetime, one meets thousands of others with whom one could have a personal relationship. Yet only a certain percentage of those, perhaps several hundred, embody the capacity to activate our unconscious imagos of self and Other. They provide the hook, Jung suggested, to catch and hold our far-flung psychic lifelines.

Remember that these imagos are comprised predominantly of our primal experiences of relationship, Mom and Dad and the dynamics between them, set in psychic granite long ago and far away. When we meet these candidates, energy is exchanged, at least from us to them, and occasionally reciprocally. When our projection hits the Other and bounces back, we experience a kind of resonance, an intimation of wholeness, and this is a form of homecoming simply because we are reconnecting with, falling in love with, ourselves.

This is not to say that the Other does not possess objective qualities, ranging from kindness and beauty to the capacity to hurt us and repeat our historic wounding, but, as already established, we do not, and cannot, really know that Other, even after prolonged exposure. Therefore what we "know" is really our experience of what Plato, in the dialogue called *The Meno,* believed all knowledge to be: re-cognition. We re-know what we once knew and forgot, or repressed, or split off, dissociated from.

This re-knowing, the re-membrance, this re-cognition, is the re-discovery of aspects of ourselves as mirrored by the Other. When the experience is reciprocal, violins play, glowing colors fill the sky, hope is renewed, the world begins afresh. And then begins the process of wearing away the mutual projections. But as nothing is more painful than the disappointment of projected hope, nothing is more intoxicating than its arousal. This arousal of hope, this shadowy origin of attraction, is what is called romance. Paradoxically, such search for reflection from the Other is also the dynamic of narcissism, which manifests in the adult who as a child was insufficiently mirrored by a loving, affirmative parent.

One analysand reported that her narcissistic father had "fallen in love with himself" when he saw himself on videos she had filmed. He went back to Florida with a copy of those images and watched them over and over. She speculated on how her life would have been different if, when she was young, he had had a television set rather than her as a reflecting object.

Those vested deeply in the idea of romance will no doubt protest, but then they will remain enslaved to the pursuit of the illusory Magical Other. The reader groans and asks, "But is there no romance? Is there nothing that makes life interesting, exciting?" But yes, of course! And that is the wonderful side of projection.

Certainly, the words of this text will not stop projection any more than we can ever become wholly conscious. When we soberly review the history of our relationships, we are obliged to acknowledge that they began at one place and evolved to quite another. If one could stay in that permanent state of romantic excitation I suppose one would so choose, but it is not possible. (I recall someone asking the Buddhist Alan Watts why one would not remain in satori, and he replied, "Because you bloody well can't.") Psychic energy cannot be fixed; its hermetic character is forever moving, dying, disappearing, reappearing in a new place, which is why the Greeks considered Eros also the youngest of the gods. Of course joy in the Other, trust, deep caring and commitment may abide. We have a word for this continuing feeling; it is love. It is not as intoxicating or illusory as romance, but it has the potential to last.

Ultimately, the health and hope of any intimate relationship will depend on each party's willingness to assume responsibility for that vertical axis, the relationship to one's own unconscious material. Sounds logical, even easy, yet nothing is more difficult. The chief burden on any relationship derives both from our unwillingness to assume responsibility and from the immensity of the project.

It takes great courage to ask this fundamental question: "What am I asking of this Other that I ought to be doing for myself?" If, for example, I am asking the Other to be mindful of my self-esteem, I have a project waiting unaddressed. If I am expecting the Other to be the good parent and take care of me, then I have not grown up. If I am expecting the Other to spare me the rigor and terror of living my own journey, then I have abdicated from the chief task and most worthy reason for my incarnation on this earth.

Of every projection we must ask, "What does this say about me?" And what we are asking of the Other, we are obliged then to ask of ourselves. Since projections are unconscious in their origin, the need for such work usually arises only due to the suffering that follows the erosion of the projection. Yet it is through taking on the heroic task of lifting our projections off of the Other that we may best serve their interest, that is, love them. As Mahatma Gandhi once remarked, "A coward is incapable of exhibiting love; it is the prerogative of the brave." Projection, fusion, "going home," is easy; loving another's otherness is heroic. If we really love the Other as Other, we have heroically taken on the responsibility for our own individuation, our own journey. This heroism may properly be called love. St. Augustine put it this way: "Love is wanting the other to be."

This view of love expresses an oxymoronic truth, that true love is "disinterested." It not only allows the Other to be but supports their being as Other. The Swiss theologian Karl Barth defined God as "Wholly Other." Well, the Beloved too is Wholly Other. Such a respect for the Other seems obvious in theory, but in reality it must always contend with our fragile, frightened nature.

The going home project is deeply programmed in us from our traumatic onsets. But, as we see all around us, it remains the chief saboteur of intimate relationship. Thus, we are all caught between the deeply programmed desire to fuse with the Other and the inner imperative to separate, to individuate. This tension of opposites will always be present. Holding that tension, bringing it to consciousness, is the moral task of both parties in any close relationship, a task that requires conscious effort and heroic will.

When one has let go of that great hidden agenda that drives humanity and its varied histories, then one can begin to encounter the immensity of one's own soul. If we are courageous enough to say, "Not this person, nor any other, can ultimately give me what I want; only I can," then we are free to celebrate a relationship for what it *can* give.[32] The paradox lies in the fact that the Other can be a means through which one is enabled to glimpse the immensity of one's own soul and live a portion of one's individuation.

Without the otherness of the Other, we would have nothing to counter the inflated certainties and one-sidedness of ego consciousness. It we only meditated on a mountaintop for the rest of our lives, we would end up talking to ghosts, by which I mean our own disembodied psychic fragments. While this sort of conversation with oneself must eventually occur, few would undertake it without being painfully confronted with the otherness of the Other. That is the chief contribution of relationship to the process of individuation. The dialogue between self and Other is a psychodynamic from which growth comes. I am more than me because you oblige me to rise up and out of my limited consciousness to recognize you as Other, and vice versa. This is the primary way in which we can help one another to grow beyond the tension of opposites.

The encounter between two people generates the possibility of what Jung calls "the reconciling third," or transcendent function. We are more than two ones who, in fusing to become One, remain

---

[32] The Administrator of the C.G. Jung Foundation of Ontario has over her desk this sign: "The inner marriage is all very well, but it doesn't warm my feet at night."

only two; we are two ones who have also become a third. As Jung wrote,

> In nature the resolution of opposites is always an energic process: she acts *symbolically* in the truest sense of the word, doing something that expresses both sides, just as a waterfall visibly mediates between above and below.[33]

This mediating third is how relationship truly serves us, and brings us to what Jung called the symbolic life. We live the symbolic life as a direct consequence of the quality of our dialogue with the world and with the cosmos. My dialogue with you is my dialogue with the cosmos, for you carry and incarnate those same energies. You oblige me to consider, to reflect, to grow, to enlarge my sense of the possible, and thereby expand my embodiment of what the Self requires. We are asked from birth to death to become as fully as possible that which we are capable of becoming. Living in a dialectic with you, I am then living the symbolic life, which is to say, a life in depth.

The dialectic of relationship described here, this grand conversation, may indeed be the proper definition of "marriage." Many married souls do not have a grand conversation, and therefore have yet to experience the *hierosgamos*, the sacred marriage, which properly honors the other as Other and at the same time protects the absolute uniqueness of the individual partners.

Love, Relationship and Soul

We need, then, to be clear about what relationship offers. On the one hand, the erosion and withdrawal of projections obliges us to recognize our parts unknown or disowned. On the other hand, the otherness of the Other obliges the inner dialectic which can stimulate, and is necessary for, the growth of both parties. ("I am more than me with you, because of you.")

Yet there is another element here which relationship also offers. The other as Other may prove to be a window on eternity, a bridge

---

[33] *Mysterium Coniunctionis,* CW 14, par. 705.

to cosmic immensity. Such are the gist of the words addressed to his Beloved by Friedrich von Hardenburg, the late-eighteenth-century poet who in time became Novalis, known especially as the seeker of the "blue flower" of eternity:

> You are the thesis, tranquil, pale, finite, self-contained. I am the antithesis, uneasy, contradictory, passionate, reaching out beyond myself. Now we must question whether the synthesis will be harmony between us or whether it will lead to a new impossibility which we have never dreamed of.[34]

In mythological language, the wonder of the Other brings intimations of the gods as we stand in the presence of mystery. *God* is the common word we use for that mystery, and we sense the presence of God in the encounter with the Other who embodies those sacred energies of the cosmos. Who has not heard that familiar Greek maxim, "Know Thyself"? But how many know that the inner sanctum of the Temple of Apollo at Delphi was adorned with the additional admonishment, "Thou Art!"

The experience of the Other as a Thou, articulated by Martin Buber for one,[35] is the ultimate challenge of relationship. Through the grunt work of making conscious our projections, through the dialectical growth that accompanies the encounter with the Other, and from the glimpse of the Thou of the cosmos, we are enlarged by relationship without having to use it regressively.

At all moments, in any relationship, the tension of opposites is present. Where there is communion, there is separateness as well. One of the best formulations of this relational paradox was expressed by the Czech poet Rainer Maria Rilke: "I hold this to be the highest task of a bond between two people: that each should stand guard over the solitude of the other."[36] We are always solitary, even in a crowd, even in relationship. We can bring no greater gift to any

---

[34] Quoted by Penelope Fitzgerald in her novel, *The Blue Flower*, p. 56.
[35] *I and Thou.* See also Mario Jacoby, *The Analytic Encounter: Transference and Human Relationship.*
[36] *Rilke on Love and Other Difficulties*, p. 28.

relationship than ourselves, as we are, singular in solitude. Similarly, there is no greater gift we may receive from the Other. A precious sharing, then, though not a substitute for our individuation.

This understanding of relationship requires never-ending vigilance. It is so easy to regress, to impose our agenda on the Other. We will do that anyway, willy-nilly, unconsciously, without meaning to, and can only hope later to recognize what we have done. Therein lies the ethical task of relationship. We say to ourselves, "The projection I cast upon the Other, this hidden agenda, needs to be withdrawn. It can be replaced by something richer." Through the enlargement which comes from the bridges of conversation, sexuality, the pooling of aspirations and "mutually-separate" journeys, one experiences the always evolving mystery of soul.

Soul may be defined here as that energy which wants something of us, which impels us to live up to who we potentially are. Its origin and aim are mysterious, but it manifests intuitively, instinctually, in moments of insight. Relationship is sacred as an arena for the enlargement of soul. Our quest for wholeness is archetypal in character, that is, programmed at the deepest level to find meaning in chaotic experience.

The seductive lure of romantic love, which so dominates Western culture, hooks us due to the profound confusion of a projection with what it is aiming toward. We fall in love with Love, and lose the growth which soul demands. As Dante suggested, the worst inferno is to be surfeited with what we seek. Like any addict, we long to die in the Other, to be subsumed, until we who would capture and hold the object of our desire are held captive instead.

We are travelers, all and separately. We are thrown by fate into adjacent seats on a flight to the coast. In our solitude we may enhance the journey of the Other, who may likewise enhance ours. We embarked separately, we disembark separately, and we head for our appointed ends separately. We profit greatly from each other without using each other. Our projections upon the Other are inevitable; not bad, really, for they enrich the journey, but if we hold on to them they become diversions from our individual task.

For each sojourner the journey requires many deaths through departure, many losses of Other, many enlargements through suffering. As Goethe observed:

> And so long as you haven't experienced
> This: to die and so to grow,
> You are only a troubled guest
> On the dark earth.[37]

Our task is wholeness, an impossibility given our fragile, finite natures. We will attain only a portion of that largeness of soul, that attainment of being, which nature seeks through us. If we were to attain that wholeness, would the two complete spheres need each other? We need not worry about transcending need, for we shall never be so strong, so evolved. Nor is it weakness or failure to need something of the Other. But when we recall that relationship which is dominated by need is also burdened by it, that we may infantilize ourselves, parentify the Other, and fail to love them as Other, then we realize that neediness must be confronted, and replaced, by consciousness. Thus Rilke worried, "How am I to withhold my soul / that it not impinge on yours?"[38] We need not worry that we shall evolve so much as to become wholly self-sufficient, but if we did, even then the otherness of the Other would facilitate growth and the enhancement of consciousness.

Our bodies, minds and souls commune through conversation, sexuality and work. We share because friendship is a good thing on a long road, but we can also bear the weight of our own journey because our soul's desire is that important to us. The disinterested love of the Other energizes; it brings a restoration of wonder, girds us for the journey and affords us glimpses of the eternal.

Think of Shakespeare's sonnets. The leitmotif running through them all is that in the face of mortality, his writing will immortalize their love, though their bodies will die. One of my favorite love poems is a rejoinder by Archibald MacLeish, "Not Marble Nor The

---

[37] "The Holy Longing," in Bly, ed., *The Soul Is Here,* p. 209.
[38] "Love Song," in Flores, ed., *An Anthology of German Poetry,* p. 390.

Gilded Monuments,"[39] which takes off on one of the best known of
Shakespeare's sonnets:

> The praisers of women in their proud and beautiful poems
> Naming the grave mouth and the hair and the eyes
> Boasted those they loved should be forever remembered
> These were lies . . . .

MacLeish names as lies those wonderful poems that promise immortality because they promise writer, subject and reader immortality, and all now molder in the grave.

> (What is a dead girl but a shadowy ghost
> Or a dead man's voice but a distant and vain affirmation
>   like dream words most)

So MacLeish bears witness to the deepest of projection's disap-
pointments, the abandonment of the evanescent Other, and the
deepest of love's hurts, loss.

> Therefore I will not speak of the undying glory of women
> I will say you were young and straight and your skin fair
> And you stood in the door and the sun was a shadow
>   of leaves on your shoulders
> And a leaf on your hair.

The poet resists the burden of writing immortally about the immortality of the mortal. He affirms the absolute radical moment of transient affirmation, the only way the human may know that he or she
was here. What, after all, is more transient that a leaf, a flash of sun,
or the Beloved?

> I will not speak of the famous beauty of dead women
> I will say the shape of a leaf lay once on your hair
> Till the world ends and the eyes are out and the mouths broken
> Look! It is there!

It is the existential moment. MacLeish was there, and he loved that
woman, and now it is gone; now they too are gone. But they *were*
there. That is as good as it gets.

---

[39] *Poems, 1924-1933*, pp. 48f.

Thus, Cupid dashes still with sagging diaper, bow and arrow. Arrows hurt, yet wounds quicken consciousness. To love the Other is to feel that wound, to care about what happens to and for that person. So many of our words, such as compassion, empathy, sympathy, come from *passio* and *pathos,* Latin and Greek words for "suffering." Thus, to open to the Other is also a willingness to open ourselves to the experience of suffering. Who is not willing to so suffer, as Goethe suggested, is only a troubled guest on the earth. To be really here, on this earth, is to experience its *gravitas.*

To use relationship as an escape from one's personal journey is to pervert relationship and to sabotage one's own calling. To care for the other as Other is to open to pain as well as joy. Both emotions can be transformative. Though we may not hold or reify either, both may engender largeness of soul. Keats said:

> Joy, whose hand is ever at his lips
> Bidding adieu; and aching pleasure nigh,
> Turning to poison while the bee month sips:
> Aye, in the very temple of Delight
> Veiled melancholy has her sovran shrine,
> Though seen of none save him whose strenuous tongue
> Can burst Joy's grape against his palate fine.[40]

When relationship is not driven by need, but by caring for the other as Other, then we are really free to experience him or her. When we let go of our projections, relinquish the "going home" project, we are free to love. When we are free to love, we are present to the mystery embodied by the Other. Without such mystery we are prisoners of childhood, trapped in the trivial. Blake said he could see eternity in a grain of sand; so we lesser mortals may glimpse the eternal in and through our Beloved. This Other, paradoxically, is a sacred vehicle toward ourselves, not because we use the Other to serve our own narcissistic ends, but because he or she serves our deepest end by remaining Wholly Other.

Love and the work of soul are inextricably entwined. The Other

---

[40] "Ode on Melancholy," in *The Norton Anthology of Poetry,* p. 663.

is not here to take care of our soul, but rather to enlarge our experience of it. Such a gift is most precious to the one enlarged. Ego consciousness understandably seeks knowledge and the relief of suffering. When we live the symbolic life through relationship, we find some knowledge, a little understanding, much suffering and a deeper capacity to love. In reality, this deeper capacity to love is a greater capacity to serve mystery. It is the movement toward *agape.* And so Rilke's "Love Song" continues:

> .... everything we are touched by, you and I,
> Draws us together as the stroke of a bow
> Mingles two strings on a single note.
> Upon what instrument have we been strung?
> And in the hands of what musician are we held?
> Oh, sweet song.[41]

Living this song is the reason we are here. The musician who plays us remains a mystery. We know we are played by forms and desires deeper than knowledge. To abandon the "going home" or Eden project is to open to the mystery of the encounter with the Other, to experience intimations of this great musician in whom and by whom we are held, and finally to free relationship for its highest service to us—the enlargement of our journey through the unfolding mystery of the otherness of the Other.

---

[41] See above, p. 62, note 38.

3

Couples
Coupling and Uncoupling

No one should ask the other
"What were you thinking?"

No one, that is,
who doesn't want to hear about the past

and its inhabitants,
or the strange loneliness of the present.
—Stephen Dunn, "After Making Love."

Out beyond ideas of wrongdoing and rightdoing.
There is a field. I'll meet you there.

When the soul lies down in that grass,
the world is too full to talk about.
Ideas, language, even the phrase each other
doesn't make any sense.
—Rumi, "Open Secret."

Since all relationships begin in projection, the course of any relationship involves the progressive erosion of projection, with concomitant surprise, confusion, dismay and sometimes anger. Then the troubles begin.

The reader thinks here, "How negative he is, how preoccupied with problems. Again, what about romance?" But remember, our subject is the reality of relationship, its psychodynamics and the conscious effort required to make it work. Romance is the hook, for sure, but in the end it will always fall short of the expectations implicit in projections and the going home agenda.

Recall the heart-felt lines addressed to his Beloved by the poet Novalis, quoted in the previous chapter ("You are the thesis, tranquil, pale, finite, self-contained . . ."). The story behind them is in-

66

structive. Novalis/von Hardenberg, in his early twenties, fell hope-
lessly in love with Sophie von Kuehn, a twelve-year-old dullard
who died of a horrible wasting disease and several surgeries two
days after she was fifteen. A typical conversation between them, as
construed by novelist Penelope Fitzgerald, is as follows. The poet
asks Sophie, "Tell me what you think about poetry." "I don't think
about it at all," she replies.[42]

Clearly, such a relationship could only depend on projection. In
his verse, Novalis tips us to the secret dynamic that exists, at least
for him, between them:

> Am I to be kept apart from her forever?
> Is the hope of being united
> With what we recognized as our own
> But could not possess completely
> Is that too to be called intoxication?[43]

What this reveals, of course, is a sense of the Other as a part of
oneself, with no inkling that such a feeling, in unrealistic. Besotted,
he gives her an engagement ring in which is inscribed: *Sophie sei
mein schütz Geist*—"Sophie, be my guardian spirit." Like Dante, he
devotes himself to the Beloved, never discerning how truly Other
she is, never discerning that he has fallen in love with Love, fallen
in love with a missing part of himself, an inner image—his anima,
as we would call it—and that they have nothing in common other
than projection.

The relationship between von Hardenberg and Sophie is rather
comic, but the underlying dynamic is common to all relationships
in the beginning, hence the later, all-too-common lament: "What on
earth did I ever see in him/her?"

As projections erode, each party may easily fall into the problem
of power. Actually, power itself is not a problem; in and of itself, it
is only the exchange or expression of energy. It becomes problematic when it is usurped by a complex, or exploited at the expense of

---

[42] *The Blue Flower*, p. 82.
[43] Ibid., p. 91.

the Other. Recall that the secret dynamic which stirs the problem of power is always fear. As we are all reluctant to recognize the place and role of our fear, to acknowledge its ubiquity and experience it without defenses, there is a natural predilection for keeping it unconscious. Thus, the traffic which floods one's sensibility, and is subsequently imposed upon the Other, is always fear based, albeit disguised in a thousand subtle permutations.

Such fears are existential and universal—the fear of abandonment, the fear of overwhelment, the fear of meaninglessness. We should not judge these fears, for they come with the territory, so to speak. But our vastly elaborate defenses against them, our reticulated reflexes which constitute the operative personality, always impose themselves upon the integrity of the Other. Just by being who we are, unavoidably who we are, with all our foibles and fragilities, we harm the Other. And we cannot help doing that, the more so as we are unconscious of who we are, what we fear, and how deeply programmed are our strategies of relationship.

The Management of Fear

Three theorists have offered some valuable ideas about the role of fear in our lives and the strategies deriving from our efforts to manage it. They are psychologists Karen Horney (1885-1952) and Fritz Riemann (1902-79), and theologian Fritz Kunkel (1889-1956).[44]

Horney suggests three basic ways in which we seek to manage our fears. In every case the fear, whether conscious or not, is projected onto the Other, no doubt a legacy, as we saw earlier, of our powerlessness in the original parent-child relationship.

The first approach is to evolve patterns of submissiveness, a turn toward the Other that tacitly acknowledges the diminution of one's own power. As is so often the case, whatever decisions we have made, most of all those that are unconscious, we have an ample

---

[44] The ideas paraphrased in this section are found in Horney, *Neurosis and Human Growth: The Struggle toward Self-Realization;* Riemann, *Grundformen der Angst* (Basic Patterns of Anxiety); Kunkel, *Selected Writings.*

supply of rationalizations to justify them. Thus the submissive strategy will be rationalized as congeniality, concern for the Other, up to and including severe co-dependence, which constitutes the annihilation of legitimate self-interest.

The second way we seek to manage fear is to bring an inherent abrasiveness or hostility to our transactions with others. This derives from early wounding and is rationalized by believing that others are caught up in their own self-interested motives. Given the "fight or flight" options nature offers us, this strategy seeks mastery over the Other, precisely in proportion to one's fear of that Other. All controlling or abusive partners are testifying to their own fearfulness. Yet, getting the abuser to look at what he or she may fear is a very tall task.

One study indicated that about 16% of males were overtly abusive to their partners. For career police officers the study found a figure as high as 40%, perhaps because a macho profession, with all the accouterments of power, seems especially attractive to those who are most psychologically insecure. Still another study indicated that therapy with abusers often backfired because it stirred up their insecurities and they became even more violent as a defense against their own fear. Bullies are too cowardly to look at their fears. Only those who felt shame at their behavior had a positive therapeutic prognosis. Normally, abusers do not voluntarily enter therapy because it would oblige them to face these issues. Indeed, the prognosis in therapy is never favorable for those who have not entered it willing to face what must be faced.

Controlling partners are least likely to change because their investment in their defense against the fear of the Other is greatest of all. Passive-aggression is a study in itself, whereby one fears the power of the Other and then must act covertly so as not to activate that Other's power. The passive-aggressive personality will often be seen in the procrastinator, the one who indicates a willingness to do a task or meet a responsibility but never gets to it, or the one who makes cutting remarks and, when challenged, asks why you took that seriously—"Can't you take a joke?"

The third defense against fear of the Other is of course flight—avoidance, isolation or emotionally hiding out even while physically present. This strategy is widespread and may not be overtly recognized because it too can be rationalized—as introversion, preoccupation with other activities, or simple blandness. A refusal to share oneself with the Other, the refusal of openness, the refusal of emotional honesty, the denial of intimacy, all are common forms of avoidance and, again, are based on the fear that immediacy in relationship makes one too vulnerable. The avoidant person ignores the resources which the adult has acquired and stays stuck at the level of the powerless child.

Horney identifies these strategies of coping with fear as submissiveness, power and distancing. Interestingly, she also identifies love as a way of dealing with fear. As we have often been told by depth psychologists and theologians, the opposite of love is not hate but fear. The capacity to affirm the Other requires an enlargement of soul to stand up against the fearfulness which is our condition. To love the Other, with all the Other's presumed power to hurt us, requires a substantial amplitude of soul, an enlargement of one's sense of self, so that one is not so precariously at risk. This is what Aristotle meant by the "magnanimous" person, one with a large enough sense of self to not only allow the Other to be Other, but to be open to whatever power, and capacity for wounding us, the Other may have. Until one can risk this kind of soulfulness, one cannot be said to be able to love.

Fritz Riemann similarly identifies the substratum of fear that courses beneath the personality and haunts relationships. He describes four primal fears:

1. The fear of nearness obliges distancing. In its extreme form it is a schizoid splitting off from the Other.

2. The fear of distance occasions an existential depression, which may go undiagnosed, so deep is its course. The depression derives from the absence of the Other, the terror of abandonment.

3. The fear of change obliges one to be obsessive-compulsive, to seek control, if not of the Other, then of those circumstances that

offer the illusion of control, such as one's own body image, the tidiness of one's house, or a frantic attention to closure in all matters, whether important or mundane.

4. The fear of permanence, which means the too-closeness of the Other—that is, the fear of engulfment—occasions what Riemann calls hysteria. In this sense, hysteria is the capacity to dissociate, to transfer one's fear into the body, to remain affectively flat or inappropriate, or simply to be "not there." After all, if one is "not there," one can't be hurt, can one?

Again, each of these fears is primal. They are not only endemic, but especially charged by the vicissitudes of individual biographies. This child's experience versus that of another child will set in motion a compensatory strategy for dealing with the wounds to self and the transactions with the Other. As we saw before, we tend to identify who we are with our strategic attitudes and behaviors. We become what we think and how we act, even if both thought and behavior are largely unconscious. While it may seem reductionist to attribute so much of the adult's behavior to such childhood wounding and reflexive response, any therapist will attest that each analysand has certain core ideas of self and Other, with specific strategies deriving from them. These largely unconscious strategies are the chief source of our repetitive patterns, our self-defeating choices and the harm we bring to our relationships.

It is very hard not to see oneself as the byproduct of one's personal history. But there is an inner energy which seeks something larger from us. And so at some point, each of us is obliged to say, "I am not only what happened to me; I am also what I choose to become." By the time one has entered therapy as an adult, however, such reflexive strategies are not only deeply programmed, they are also identified with in one's defense against primal fears, and commonly rationalized as, for instance, "simply who I am," or "the way I have always been." If it is difficult to have a conscious relationship to our own psychological history, how difficult it is, then, to have a relationship with the Other, not only the Other as Other, but even that Other which is our own soul.

Theologian Fritz Kunkel identifies four fundamental types who fall into the problem of power:

1. There is the one who would be the "star," longs for and solicits the admiration of others, thereby seeking external validation for what is not felt within.

2. The "clinging vine" is dependent, having resigned responsibility for self, seeking validation through an identification with the will of the Other.

3. The "turtle" seeks protection and security at all costs. This person will marry for money, identify with the social position of the Other, take the path of least resistance in avoiding the demands of personal choice.

4. The last is the "Nero" type, one who overtly seeks power, again in direct proportion to his or her feelings of inadequacy. This is the person most identified with persona, the one who needs to have the title on the door, the key to the executive washroom, the flashy car, etc., in order to demonstrate power, and with that power, assume enhanced self-worth.

Each of these types, and we may all recognize such tendencies in ourselves, is caught in the problem of power, stuck in the developmental process. If our task is to become ourselves, then each of these tendencies represents an impediment. Driven always by our fears, these tendencies arise from, and in turn reinforce, a false sense of self. Each represents the place where growth is blocked. Obviously, only if one's fear can be made conscious can one expect to evolve.

Kunkel considers this stuckness to be an off-shoot of egocentricity. Jungian analyst John Sanford summarizes Kunkel's paradigm of the capacity for growth:

> There are three basic experiences through which our egocentricity can be changed: through suffering, through the recognition of a power greater than our own will at work in our lives, and by coming to care for someone other than oneself.[45]

---

[45] *The Man Who Wrestled with God,* p. 26.

By "egocentricity," Kunkel means that we are "wound-identified," that is, stuck at the level of our wounding. Paradoxically, growth comes when we suffer, for suffering quickens consciousness and generally requires the enlargement of the personality to assimilate the pain. Secondly, the radical encounter with the Other can also pry us out of our ego-bound position. This is what the mystic experiences. This is what constitutes *metanoia*, a transformative experience, and it is what lies at the heart of all Twelve Step programs—the encounter with a Higher Power.

One analysand told me that she had never understood the idea of a Higher Power, as she thought of herself as nonreligious. But one day after an AA meeting she realized that the "Higher Power" in her life had the shape of a bottle. That was way too small for her, she thought, and then she was moved to apprehend the Higher Power behind her erstwhile Higher Power.

Lastly, Kunkel affirms the transformative character of love, the caring for the Other that lifts us up and out of our ego-bound constrictions. The willingness to sacrifice ourselves for the well-being of another is transformative. The self-sacrifice of a parent for a child, for example, opens the parent to a more capacious life. The fears which bind one to the past, which limit one's growth, are powerful indeed. The sociopath, whose whole personality is organized around fear and as a defense against it, cannot love and therefore cannot grow.

The power of love is found most in its triumph over fear. Where fear prevails, love is not. Given the ubiquity of fear, the move to love is a considerable challenge. Only those who can face their fears, live with ambiguity and ambivalence, can find that personal empowerment which then makes possible love of the Other.

As noted earlier, usually by the time a couple arrives in therapy a lot of mutual wounding has occurred. The projections have worn away; the going home project has surfaced, with attendant disillusionment and anger; they are both bleeding from the thorns on the rose of love. Each party feels justified, believes his or her cause righteous, and is certain that an unbiased third party will confirm that belief. Each expects the therapist to hear the blow by blow account, assign a score and declare a winner. Each feels the Other has much to account for. Bitterness and animosity hang in the air. Since both are on the whole unconscious, it is difficult indeed to shift the focus from blame to self-examination, individual responsibility and the need for personal growth.

Ultimately one is obliged to become conscious of and responsible for some basic principles of relationship. Therein lies the possibility of transformation. Sometimes only one person takes on the task, and the other stays stuck. At that point, the former may grow into greater independence and leave the tacit contract, and often the relationship itself, behind.

Four Principles of Relationship

The principles that follow are all predicated on the thesis of this book, namely that one can achieve no higher or better relationship with the Other than one has achieved with oneself.

1. What we do not know about ourselves (the unconscious project), or will not face in ourselves (the shadow), will be projected onto the Other.

2. We project our childhood wounding (personal pathology), our infantile longing (the narcissistic going home agenda), and our individuation imperative onto the Other.

3. Since the Other cannot, and should not, bear responsibility for our wounds, our narcissism or our individuation, the projection gives way to resentment and the problem of power.

4. The only way to heal a faltering relationship is to render our going home project conscious and take personal responsibility for our individuation.

Let us examine each of these principles in some detail.

1) What we do not know about ourselves will be projected onto the Other.

We cannot be conscious of that of which we are unconscious. Jung even said that all our psychological theories are forms of confession wherein our own material will be found.[46] Relationships are forever clogged, blocked, stymied by the phenomenon which therapists call "transference," which occurs because our psyche functions analogously. That is to say, the psyche is an historical reality. We carry our entire personal history within us. The present is always being "read" through the lens of that history. The psyche says, in effect, "Where or when have I been here before? What previous experience does this feel like? What is the analogue?" Thus, it is very difficult to simply be in the moment, because this moment is itself viewed through the prism of history.

Obviously, the experience of intimacy will activate one's entire prior experience of the intimate Other, especially the primal relationships with the parents. Thus, the vulnerability, the neediness, the strategies of those first fortuitous couplings will always be present, always informing and often sabotaging the present. Indeed, even the imago of the beloved Other is highly contaminated by the parental complexes. It is not that we seek our mother or father in the Beloved; it is that as we enter the precinct of intimacy, the analogues of prior experience with the Primal Others are evoked and play out their historically conditioned schemas.

Similarly, what we wish not to acknowledge about ourselves— our narcissism, our selfishness, our rage and so on, all the shadow stuff—gets repressed and/or projected onto the Other. One woman in therapy with me had a husband with a highly restricted range of emotion. Thus, he would provoke her to anger, to sorrow, to conflict, so as to experience his own emotional reality—and then blame her for being so emotional. In such ways does the shadow make its presence known in a relationship.

The shadow, this "heavy bear who goes with me," this "stupid clown of the spirit's motive,"[47] is always present and enormously resistant to discovery. The ego is threatened by the shadow's autonomy on the one hand, and the largeness of its threat to one's

---

[46] "Freud and Jung: Contrasts," *Freud and Psychoanalysis,* CW 4, par. 774.
[47] See above, p. 30.

self-image on the other. Our understandable resistance to our shadow stuff, however, becomes the source of many of the qualities we project upon our fractious partners, as well as the chief source of dissatisfaction in the relationship. And remember, where there is a couple there are *two* shadows. . . .

Making the unconscious conscious, owning our own charged material, is an extraordinarily difficult task, no matter how willing we may be. We make the unconscious conscious by examining our patterns, not only in the present but in our whole history of relationships. We must watch for when and where we are most charged, that is, times when complexes most commonly surface. When our affective response is intense and our rationalizations plentiful, we can be sure that complexes are at work. Being in an intimate relationship is a bit like asking someone to join hands with us, but only after walking across a field in which we have planted mines.

Blaming our partner for stepping on mines we have laid is where most couples are when they walk into therapy that first hour. In addition, the person who quite possibly knows us best, perhaps better than we know ourselves (at least our shadow side), will be that very partner. While it is threatening and humbling to hear the Other's candid observations—and distrustful of such disclosure as we may be—the value of the partner's contribution to our self-knowledge cannot be overemphasized.

2) We project our childhood wounding and our individuation imperative onto the Other.

The human estate is precarious indeed. As Pascal noted in his seventeenth-century *Pensées,* we are but a fragile reed, and yet a thinking reed capable of writing the Brandenburg concerto, creating a concentration camp or imagining our own demise.

No one escapes pathology, for no one remains unwounded. *Pathos,* as noted earlier, derives from the Greek word for suffering. Psychopathology may then literally be translated as "the expression of the soul's suffering." It is not whether or not one is wounded, but how deeply, and, more important, what adaptations we have made as a result.

The operative personality is both a set of precepts about self and Other, and a set of reflexive strategies to manage the energies that traverse the gap between. The primary motive of those strategies is the management of anxiety, and in the context of relationship this derives from the existential distress the Other may occasion in us by flooding our boundaries or abandoning us. Thus, it is not life's inevitable wounding that damages our relationships, but the precepts and stratagems we bring from our personal histories and impose upon the Other. Just as we wish to love the Other, and be loved in return, so we bring our history to them. How could we not? Obviously, not all our history is the saga of suffering, or we would be unable to bond with others at all, but the good stuff takes care of itself. It's the bad stuff that contaminates our relationships.

Moreover, it is in the nature of our condition that we long for the Other. As life began with the primal separation from the Other, so we seek, forever, to return. In our age we may even be said to have a culture of longing. We long for the gods who went underground. We long for connections, for fixes. We are all addicted, seeking connection through chemical substances, money and power, and most of all through the Magical Other. We long for nurturance, for safe harbor, for completion.

So it has always been, but our culture longs even more, perhaps because of the diminution of those connections of family and myth-preserving tribal institutions which served people in previous times. The virtual disappearance of those connective tissues has left us stranded on the narrow isle of narcissism, alone, afraid, self-absorbed and longing for some Other to save us.

Perhaps no modern poem better expresses this promotion of the Other to such a high calling than Matthew Arnold's "Dover Beach." After comparing the ebbing tide at Dover with the recession of the Age of Faith, Arnold concludes that all agencies of connection and salvation are exhausted but one, namely his Beloved. The Beloved may be counted upon, will remain true even as they are obliged to remain

> ... here as on a darkling plain
> Swept with confused alarm of struggle and flight,
> Where ignorant armies clash by night.[48]

Arnold was not alone. As suggested earlier, it may not be off the mark to say that in our time more people look for salvation through relationship than in houses of worship.

The twin conditions for growth require first that we take responsibility for our journey. No matter what the historic wounding, we must now and forever assume responsibility for our choices. Secondly, we must also be able to internalize, that is, be able to see that one's life is generated by choices whose dynamics derive from within. We are obliged to reflect, to ask, "Where in me does this come from? What does it hit in my history? What does it feel like? What hidden source is creating repetitive patterns in my life?"

These questions are necessary for personal growth, yet they are not commonly asked, even by those who voluntarily go into therapy. Nor are they held in high esteem by our extraverted, materialistic culture. Taking responsibility for one's journey is part and parcel of individuation. The individual's task is *to be* individual, to bring to fruition that experiment Nature is making through us.

All this will be obvious to some, but the awe which our own journey inspires is intimidating to many. We are afraid to be ourselves, afraid to be wholly responsible. Surely there is an Other somewhere who can spare us this burden. Surely there is a social institution, a personal God, a Magical Other who will lift from us the terrible weight of our freedom and responsibility; or perhaps one imagines the answer is in a book yet to be read, as in this candid admission by Jungian analyst Daryl Sharp:

> I used to have a fantasy that somewhere there was a Big Book of collective wisdom called *What To Do When*. It contained the prescribed solution to all life's problems. Whenever you found yourself in a conflict you could just look it up in the book and do what it said. Such a fantasy comes from the father complex. If there were a book

---

[48] *The Norton Introduction to Poetry*, p. 91.

like that, I wouldn't have to think for myself—I'd just do what was laid down by tradition.[49]

Jung observed that "neurotic suffering is an unconscious fraud and has no moral merit, as has real suffering."[50] Elsewhere he writes that a neurosis "must be understood, ultimately, as the suffering of a soul which has not discovered its meaning."[51] Just so, we are obliged to take responsibility for our suffering and the task of meaning which it occasions. We all, from time to time, wish to shuffle this mortal coil off onto the shoulders of the Other. In so doing, we are deeply human, yet do profound damage to our relationships. Taking responsibility for ourselves is the greatest terror of our journey, and the greatest gift we can bring to the Other.

3) Projection gives way to resentment and the problem of power.

While the chief fantasy of our culture of longing is to find a Magical Other to ease the burden of our individuation, no one can ever do that. And if we were to find someone who could, we would then be bound in a horribly regressive relationship, one in which the partners are rule-bound, infantile and stuck. We all know relationships like that, and they are not a pretty sight. Both partners have to be wound-identified, that is, not only wounded, as we all are, but psychologically defined by their wounds, locked into the splinter mythologies of their pathology. At least one partner must be extremely and overtly needy, with the other needing to be needed—thus co-dependence, a state wherein both are emotionally constricted, developmentally stuck, fused in the psychologically naive fantasy that the Other can truly take care of them. Welcome to "happy neurosis island," as one of Jung's patients described it.[52]

Once I saw a woman for an analytic session shortly after her

---

[49] *Jungian Psychology Unplugged: My Life As an Elephant,* p. 50.
[50] "Analytical Psychology and Education," *The Development of the Personality,* CW 17, par. 154.
[51] "Psychotherapists or the Clergy," *Psychology and Religion,* CW 11, par. 497.
[52] "The Psychology of the Transference," *The Practice of Psychotherapy,* CW 16, par. 374.

husband had died of a sudden heart attack. She asked, in all seriousness, "Now, who will get up in the middle of the night with me when I have to go to the bathroom?" When I suggested to this woman, who was not physically handicapped, that she was finally obliged to care for herself, she left and did not come back.

The search for fusion regularly gives rise to various symptoms. Our own psyche knows what is right for us, knows what is developmentally demanded. When we use the Other to avoid our own task, we may be able to fool ourselves for awhile, but the soul will not be mocked. It will express its protest in physical ailments, activated complexes and disturbing dreams. The soul wishes its fullest expression; it is here, as Rumi expressed it, "for its own joy."

Let's continue the fantasy of finding an Other willing to carry our individuation task for us. Well, in time that Other would grow to resent us, even though he or she was a willing signatory to the silent contract. That resentment would leak into the relationship and corrode it. No one is angrier than someone doing "the right thing" and secretly wishing for something else. No one becomes more frustrated than the one who washes a mate's laundry at the expense of his or her own.

Most commonly, as we lay our primal parental projections on our partners, and find them not carrying the burden as we wish, we grow puzzled, angry, disillusioned. "Why don't you make me feel good about myself?" we ask, usually unconsciously but sometimes straight out. "Why don't you meet my needs?" There the Other sits, obnoxiously and frustratingly Other, not at all who we had thought him or her to be. In the beginning we loved the otherness of the Other. Now it drives us up the wall. He, or she, must have changed! How easy to feel betrayed, to fall into resentment and the use of power. Jump ship? No, couldn't ever, just think of the kids. And so, through tactics of dependence or anger or control, mixed with emotional and sexual withdrawal, we try to force the Other back into our original, imaginary mold.

Such strategies constitute the usual second phase of a relationship, when the truly otherness of the Other begins to emerge and the projections that made the relationship possible in the first place slowly dissolve. Rarely is this progression welcomed as a chance for personal growth, or as an opportunity to know who, really, is the Other, if not the one we thought we'd hooked up with. Quite the contrary, we resent the formerly loved one for having now, maliciously, become unlovable. We retaliate by using power. Again, power itself is neutral, being simply the exchange of energy between people. It can be benign or malignant, healing or hurtful— but it is always there.

When couples fall into the problem of power it becomes very easy to be critical of the Other. We suddenly see all their flaws of character and annoying behaviors. We are prone to have an affair, actually or fantasized, because the archaic need for the Magical Other stirs and the libido looks elsewhere. It will not take long for such primal material to find an object on which to land. One would not be so tempted if the primary Other were in fact serving the terms of the tacitly contracted going home project. Since he or she is not doing so, we project the archaic material onto another Other, seeking renewal, the recovery of energy, the revival of hope. Clearly, few who have affairs intend to leave their marriage or injure their partners, but the frequency of such events is ample testimony to the power of the archaic, unconscious Eden project.

So, the problem of power is implicit in all relationships and explicit in many. Its ubiquity speaks to the universality of our existential wounding. Fueled by frustrated need, we turn on the Other to bring about their compliance. The violent partner is the least capable of conscious reflection and is profoundly terrified at the loss of control over the Other. That Other might hurt them as they have been hurt before, engulfing them or abandoning them. It has been said that violence is the language of the inarticulate. So the abusive partner uses violence because he or she cannot consciously approach the experience of primal wounding which could lead to intrapsychic healing.

In exercising power over the Other, whether consciously or not, we deny their individuality, violate their souls and push them further and further away. All couples will err, stumble into power. It is inevitable. But some will recover and repair the damage, rendering the relationship more satisfying because less burdened, more real.

Once again, the concept of the shadow is very helpful here. Like the complex, it is never exhausted as a rich source of reflection and learning. We could define the shadow functionally as "that within myself with which I am uncomfortable." As we tend to avoid what makes us uncomfortable, we are seldom conscious of the way we enact sundry power ploys. We may sense our partner's shadowy expressions of power and draw back, accede or resist, but seldom are we free to admit our own power stratagems. Thus, the problem of power is always present, as is the shadow. It is not a question of whether the shadow is at work in a relationship, but how conscious we are of it and how deleterious its effects.

Perhaps the most damaging aspect of the will to power is its employment in coercing the Other into sparing us our own responsibilities. Just as we once wished the protection and security of the parent, so as adults we look to the Other to protect us, spare us, lead us. Since this enormous hope is essentially unconscious, the problem of power is our problem; we are owned by the shadowy intricacies of power. As our human condition is vulnerable, so the problem of power is ubiquitous. As our relationships are always replicating our history, so the wounds and narcissism of that history are always imposing themselves upon us and our partners.

To recognize this power dilemma is not to be pessimistic about the possibility of relationship; it is to open the door to freeing self and Other to be who each is meant to be. It is to open both to the possibility of something called love.

4) The only way to heal relationship is to take full responsibility for one's own individuation.

What a disappointment, how unromantic—the Other was not put on earth to serve or take care of me, protect me from my life! What a profound disappointment—almost as great as that loss of Edenic connection we call our birth, or our first tenuous tumble to the truth of our mortality. We are it, apparently. Alone, and on the road.

Yet we are not wholly alone. The road is filled with others like us. We may offer each other encouragement, compassion, even great assistance, but we cannot take on another's journey any more than another can die our death for us. If they cannot die our death, why should they live our lives? Is not the meaning of being here tied to our becoming whatever the gods, or nature, intended?

Individuation demands an energy larger and tougher than the narcissism of the Eden project. It is humbling, terrifying at times, and always an invitation to the enlargement of meaning. Becoming ourselves is not the work of ego, though ego can support or hinder it. Ego may also be steamrollered aside when the individuation instinct will no longer be denied, as many of us have learned. Though it all remains a great mystery, we are meant to be here, on the road, journeying toward maturity, east of Eden. If we understood it all, the mystery would be reduced to being only an artifact of ego. Yet, as we have seen, ego is fragile, terrified, dependent and longing for that Other. Accepting the journey obliges one to accept fear, and to let go of our chief fantasies.

Relinquishing the expectation of rescue by the Other is one of the most difficult projects of our lives. Thus, central to any long-term therapy is the progressive assumption of responsibility for oneself. Fred Hahn has eloquently, forcefully, spoken of this:

> The goal of therapy is to help the patient go beyond intellectualization and rationalization and other resistive maneuvers to the point where he can move into uncharted territories to seek and find the anguish and terror of total realization and discover that he can survive. To know that life can be truly absurd and capricious; that one is not omnipotent; that without magic as the ultimate defense, there is pain at times which hurts more than words can describe. And after the grief and the mourning, not only for the lost objects of one's fantasies, but for the fantasies and illusions themselves, to be able to live relatively without illusion. To know Time as a friend as well as an enemy. To recognize that happiness is not a condition, but an ephemeral and precious experience, that if one lives without illusion one must impart meaning to one's life; that hope must replace ex-

pectations and demands; that activity must replace passivity; that realistic hope must be directed towards the expansion and growth of one's potentialities, which implies experiencing more richly both sorrow and joy. That the gates to that Eden of infancy are closed, barred by angels with fiery swords. That mother is dead, forever, and ever, and ever.[53]

That about sums it up. The "mother" to whom Hahn refers in the last sentence is the mother complex, the charged energy within us which longs for security, succor and sanctuary. The Edenic state, preconscious fusion with the Other, is no longer tenable. What courage it takes, then, just *to be*. Yet, it is in answering the summons to such a courage that we most help our partners. We relieve them of our impossible Eden project. We share with them the best person we can be—what a gift! And when we live our own journey, freeing our partners for the rigors of their task in life, then we most care for them, most honor them. This may properly be called love, though it is light years away from being "in love."

We should have different words for the disparate realities we call love, but they seem inextricably fused in the popular mind, perhaps irredeemably. The love I speak of here is heroic; it is freeing to both parties, transformative rather than regressive. As finite beings, we are seldom up to its demands, but when we are, our journeys take on depth and substance.

The above four principles constitute the continuous course and challenge of intimacy. We are all familiar with the first three steps. Who has not fallen in love, experienced frenzies of expectation, in time found the Other wanting, and then become enmeshed in conflict? It is a familiar paradigm. Some of us, some of the time, struggle with the fourth principle, with what it asks of us—to give up our deepest longing for homecoming—its challenge to grow up, take responsibility, to be an adult instead of a child. We always carry that frightened child within, and the power of the adult we seek to become must be balanced against the demands of the child.

---

[53] "On Magic and Change."

But when we can comfort our frightened child, stand watch on the ramparts of our own soul, then we may experience transformation.

Joseph Campbell expressed this goal in typically direct fashion:

> I think one of the problems in marriage is that people don't realize what it is. They think it's a long love affair and it isn't. Marriage has nothing to do with being happy. It has to do with being transformed, and when the transformation is realized it is a magnificent experience. But you have to submit. You have to yield. You have to give. You can't just dictate.[54]

So relationship is not about happiness, then? It's about transformation? Happiness, were it a fixable state, might be very fine indeed, but it is never fixable—it remains transient, always slipping from our grasp. Though the original projection onto the Other offers the fantasy of happiness, reality cannot sustain the promise. Once the Other is revealed as really Other, not just the carrier of our projections, the troubles begin.

Transformation is about enlargement, and enlargement generally comes only from suffering. Stop and reflect on growth experiences. Invariably they arise out of conflict and loss, for consciousness only comes from the tension of opposites. Discovering the otherness of the Other can lead to disinterested love, the energy which incarnates through caring for the other as Other, valuing and celebrating their otherness.

For those fortunate enough to find disinterested love, relationship is transformative. We are far richer after, even with loss and conflict, than we were before. For such richness we may be grateful. We may even come to bless those who have most hurt us, for they have most contributed to our transformation. We may even love them, allowing them to be who they are, even as we struggle to be ourselves on the journey toward our own destined end.

---

[54] *This Business of the Gods,* p. 78.

4
Becoming Conscious of Eros Wounds

Just as the tree is bent by wind and time, and the tendril curves toward the light, so our life force, our eros, is sculpted by our experience. All our personal distortions of perception come to us through the workings of fate.

We have one set of chromosomes rather than another, one set of parents, one culture to serve or reject. Each of these fortuities twists and turns eros and sends it off on missions to heal, missions to replicate wounding, missions to transcend the dictates of fate itself. We are, generally speaking, unconscious of these missions. When we have lived long enough to create patterns of behavior, and have perhaps emerged a little from our unconsciousness, and if we have also attained sufficient ego strength to reflect honestly, only then can we see the flotsam and jetsam encircling our lives due to these missions. Sometimes we will feel humiliated, sometimes defeated; seldom can we honestly conclude that we knew all along what was happening.

Five case illustrations will demonstrate the shaping of eros and the lives which emerge from that primal imprint.

The Boy Who Failed His Mother

As a child Gregory had learned what really mattered in life—it was what mattered to his mother. His father knew his place—to earn what money he could. When he was ten, Gregory walked all day in a snowy Philadelphia trying to sell subscriptions to the *Saturday Evening Post*. When he returned home, weary, frozen, hungry, he reported to his mother than he had not managed to sell a single one. She ordered him back out into the dark until he could make a sale.

From memories like this, Gregory derived his philosophy of life. What mattered was what mattered to the boss, to Mother. She valued money and power, and people who had both. From such a lens, derived from a woman scarred by poverty and want in her own childhood, he too set his sights on money and power. From his unmet childhood need for unconditional acceptance, he evolved an operative personality which led him to great worldly achievement in what may be called the first adulthood. From his twenties to his fifties, he achieved enormous financial success and rose to be president of a major corporation. He married out of obligation, to a woman for whom he had little affection. He dutifully fathered two children. He severely abused alcohol, had recurrent affairs and frequented prostitutes on a regular basis. Money and power were the name of the game, and he had plenty of both. He had status, privilege, toys, mobility and the apparent respect of others. His money even bought him what he thought was love. "Back then," he said, "I believed the women I purchased really did love me."

When Gregory realized that the price he was paying for his alcoholism was greater than the gains, he joined AA and stayed steadfastly sober. Feeling then the need to take a measure of control over his life, he concurrently divorced his wife, stopped seeing prostitutes, and decided to enjoy life by playing a lot of golf. Simultaneously, he embarked upon three love affairs. As a measure of his sobriety and sincerity, he was completely candid with each of his three partners about the existence of the others. Each, grudgingly, tolerated the *ménage à quatre*.

It was not a crisis that brought him to therapy. His announced reason was essentially curiosity about himself, though one may surmise that the Self had some larger intent. He considered marriage a trap, a loss of freedom, and had no intention of ever making that mistake a second time. Although all three of his relationships had a sexual component, sex as such seemed peripheral. Each mistress was a somewhat younger professional woman whom Gregory supported with both money and encouragement. He played the role of mentor for all three—carried their animus, we might say— though that was not his conscious intent. While each of the women profited in several ways from their relationship, each sought a more permanent commitment, which Gregory was unwilling to grant.

By now one can discern the lineaments of wounded eros—as a child he lacked unconditional warmth from his mother, and learned quickly to work for what she wanted—money and power. At the same time he had to avoid commitment to someone who would not be there for him.

As we have seen, behavior is always logical, as long as we can discern the eros wound from which it comes. All that follows then flows *psycho*-logically out of the desire to treat the wound. Gregory had married out of duty, had children out of duty, had even been successful out of duty, sought "love" from mother surrogates, and anesthetized the pain of his inner woman, or anima, with vodka. He certainly would not wish to place himself back in the sort of relationship where he would be hurt again.

While each of the three women with whom Gregory was involved did express affection for him, none of those relationships could develop because his attitudes and expectations were fueled by the dynamics, the psycho-logic, of his childhood experience of his mother. Each relationship carried a dual, contradictory dynamic for Gregory. His unconscious agenda was to make himself so valuable to each of these women that they would need him, desire him and be there for him, and yet he refused commitment, for therein lay the profound abyss of his childhood fear of being abandoned.

This transferential dynamic is common to all relationships; it is only a matter of fate's infinite capacity for subtle variation that produces the range of relational styles. Any therapist, especially those who work with couples, will recognize the unconscious dynamics governing relationships, ever fueled by those first ones, long ago and far, far away. Gregory could have chosen Walt Whitman's reputed line for his life's motto: "Dark Mother always gliding near with soft feet."

Gregory has come to recognize the patterns. All that power, all that money—all acquired to protect the child who failed to sell a subscription to the *Saturday Evening Post*. That child still wanders this world feeling that he hasn't yet met the requirements for being loved. Gregory now knows that what he really seeks is not power and money but unconditional love. He will not visit the bottle, will not visit prostitutes, because he knows he will only leave lonely again, unfulfilled, unmet by the Other. He wants now to know, perhaps for the first time in his life, the grace of being loved for who he is, without having to prove himself worthy. His need is like Paul Tillich's definition of grace: "Accept the fact that you are accepted, despite the fact that you are unacceptable."[55]

Gregory is now reexamining each of his relationships, focusing on the similarity of their hidden agendas. While consciously he does not wish his partners to be his mother, the style of these relationships are driven by that old wound. He is poised on the brink of knowing what he really wants, what so much of his outwardly successful but inwardly unsatisfying life has been about. The wound to the child's eros has driven the adult's life, as it does for us all.

The measure of our possible healing is the extent of our willingness and capacity to face such wounds, our unconscious patterns, our deepest desires. Gregory is ready to accept an enlarged concept of relationship with an Other, and he now knows this is possible only through an enlarged relationship with himself. The little boy he was, still part of him, may forever roam the wintry streets of Philadelphia seeking somehow to please his mother, but his needs will no longer automatically rule Gregory's life.

The Dark River God of the Blood

Steven was in his fifties, married to the same woman for twenty-five years. In our first few sessions he spoke of a general malaise and thoughts of a career change. He told me he loved his wife and cared deeply for her well-being, but had lost any sexual desire for her several years before, a loss they both regretted.

Like Gregory, Steven had come into therapy willingly but unclear as to why, simply acknowledging that a conversation with himself was long overdue. While he thought that the general malaise from which he suffered might indicate a needed career change,

---

[55] *The Shaking of the Foundations*, p. 162.

he also sensed that he had an appointment with his inner woman that he was obliged to keep.

Inhibited sexual desire is not uncommon among men in their fifties. It can easily be blamed on fatigue, diminished libido due to age, and/or the mundane routine that affects any relationship. But also this diminishment of desire may occur when the man's partner, now aging along with him, is plumper, more maternal, has graying hair and so on. Without his knowing it, the image of his partner hits the old mother imago which he carries from childhood. All that "mother" represents to him may be desirable, but at the same time it activates the incest taboo.

The fear of incest is really the fear of powerlessness and regression into infantile dependence. In the face of this transferred power, the Other is unconsciously experienced as threatening the child's autonomy. This can be one reason why many men who divorce are prone to pick up with a younger woman rather than one more appropriate to their own age and experience. Another reason is that the man who has paid no attention to the development of his anima will naturally seek his own emotional level in an outer woman.

Steven's father was generally in the background during his childhood, while his mother played the dominant role in the formation of his conscious and unconscious values. In addition, a strong religious upbringing had inculcated pronounced superego values. So, unlike Gregory, Steven would not consider a trip to the dark side of substances or frolics with ladies of the night. During the early years he plowed his eros into parenting and career, and, after the children moved away, into career alone. These investments of energy seemed the right thing at the time, but they estranged him more and more from himself and from his wife. The bending of the slim reed of eros directed Steven toward the values of middle-class America, but essentially severed him from the archetypal energies which course below the surface of relationships.

One day, in discussing his sexual withdrawal from his wife, I asked Steven how she viewed the loss. He said he didn't know, but that she would probably do a lot of praying that matters would be resolved. To spare her feelings, he had blamed it all on the side effects of Prozac, which had been prescribed by his physician for a low-grade depression. He assured his wife that there was nothing wrong with her. We concluded that perhaps her prayers were being answered tangentially, as he was now willing to acknowledge the loss for both of them and seek to understand its meaning.

Pushing the paradox further, I suggested that he had somehow forgotten, or never been taught, that sexual communion was a sacred gift, religious in character. While neither of them would neglect an overtly religious task, they had forgotten the transcendent aspect of sexuality.[56] When Jung observed that a neurosis is like an offended god, he meant that a god is the dramatization of a certain archetypal energy, the neglect or abuse of which occasions considerable suffering. To neglect or offend a god is ultimately to wound ourselves, for the gods represent the forces of nature that course through us. While maintaining faithful service to outer religious values, Steven and his wife had lost contact with the gods that move nature and history. Neurosis, in the Jungian view, represents self-estrangement, therefore estrangement from the gods within. To neglect the chthonic gods while serving the spiritual ones is to commit an unintentional offense against the Divine. My feeling was that Steven's depression stemmed at least in part from this offense of self-alienation, which medication would only mask.

I suggested to Steven that perhaps he and his wife needed to search for the god to be found in sexuality. The idea seemed to intrigue him. His task was on the one hand to recover a relationship to his own depths and those within his wife, and to neutralize the blocking effect of his stern mother complex.

"Perhaps you need to find and follow what Rilke called the dark 'river god of the blood,' "[57] I said. "The gods ask that we respect

---

[56] For an exposition of the connection between spirituality and passionate love, see Nancy Qualls-Corbett, *The Sacred Prostitute: Eternal Aspect of the Feminine.*

[57] "It is one thing to sing the beloved. Another, alas, / to sing that hidden guilty river god of the blood." (The Third Elegy, lines 1-2, *Duino Elegies,* p. 21).

them. If you consider yourself religious, then this god too must be served. When you neglect such a powerful divinity, it may avenge itself elsewhere in your life."

Steven also had the implicit task to broaden his view of what was religious. The higher powers are powers, indeed, but so are the lower ones, and they will not be mocked. This perspective was liberating for Steven. Because such contact with the river god of the blood is a spiritual calling, and leads to the enlargement of the individual, it has more power than the regressive energies of the childhood complex. Indeed, in general, to depotentiate any complex we need the energy of an imago with greater power.

Another of Steven's tasks was to examine his assumptions about his wife. He had to rediscover her as a desirable, and desiring, woman, and to see the gift of herself to him, and of himself to her, as wondrously beautiful offerings. To re-image his wife as a person willing to enter with him into religious depths, to be open and vulnerable to him, to draw him deeper into himself, was in effect re-animating his anima.

In the end, the idea that sexuality, the dark river god of the blood, is sacred, resulted in the renewal of their physical intimacy. What Steven and his wife had initially suffered as a mutual loss subsequently became theirs to experience more deeply than before.

The Abilene Paradox

The immensity of the unconscious Eden project, the effects of the secret agenda, cannot be overemphasized. It lies at the heart of our experience of our own fragility and the implicit power of the Other.

One couple came into therapy with each seeking to "fix" the Other. Joyce and Joe had reached retirement, with its long sought freedom to do whatever they wanted, and then found each other in the way. Each felt responsible for the Other, and if the Other was out of sorts, adrift, depressed or testy, each felt obliged to take greater care, to put the Other back together, so that then the partner could be there for them. Having seen them together and separately, I was impressed by the sameness of their reports, how similar were their analyses of the Other. Each, in turn, expected me to solve the problem—of the Other. I became aware that I was looking at a variation of what has been called the "Abilene paradox."

The expression was coined by Jerry Harvey, a guru of the OD (Organizational Development) profession. Harvey noted once that even though no one really wanted to drive from their west Texas town to Abilene on a miserably hot day to get ice cream, no one spoke up, and so a carload of disgruntled, irritable adults made the trek and then exploded at each other on the long road back. This phenomenon, which he titled the Abilene paradox, occurs when couples or groups have a large measure of tacit or explicit agreement but somehow wind up doing the opposite. The most chilling illustration of this was the decision process which led to the Challenger disaster in 1986. Over forty contractors indicated that conditions were not right for a launch. But after a vote was taken the mission was on, and we all know the rest.

For the next joint session with Joyce and Joe, I typed up the following list and presented it to them.

The Abilene Paradox

(How Groups or Couples Can Agree, Yet Do the Opposite)

You both agree that:

1. You love, care for, value, and wish to support the Other.
2. You believe your Other is depressed.
3. The Other is depressed for reasons you consider to be intrapsychic rather than external. (The Other has problems which he/she needs to address individually.)
4. Yet, you feel responsible for the depression of the Other.
5. You are afraid to take independent steps without the Other because you fear that would upset, anger or depress the Other.
6. You are angry and depressed at this stalemate, and partly blame the Other for it.
7. You love the Other, but feel far apart from him/her right now.
8. You expect the therapist to solve this dilemma by treating the Other's problems.

Their separate childhood histories had programmed each of them to take responsibility for the feeling state of the Other. This is always a bad idea; it burdens everyone and is no help in the end, for it seeks to spare the Other from that suffering which is the necessary prelude to growth. In reality, neither claimed to be depressed, though each diagnosed the Other as such. Both felt frustrated and angry that in their hard-won retirement freedom, they could not act independently—pursue individual interests—for fear that the partner would feel abandoned. Each, in short, was throttled by his or her own attitudes, though their feelings were being projected onto the partner. What they expected of the therapist, naturally, was to agree with their assessment and treat the Other, so that the relationship would again be agreeable.

What they did not realize was that each had to examine his or her own attitudes, the taking of too much responsibility for the Other and the making of self-constrictive choices. Only then, if ever, could the relationship evolve in an amicable way.

As Joyce and Joe listened to the items of the Abilene paradox, the accuracy of each point was agreed. With the last point they saw the paradox and roared with laughter. The tension broke, the polarization began to thaw, and the relationship moved forward. The task of therapy had been not only to point out the contradictions in their thinking, but to invite them to improve the relationship by first improving their own individual lives.

The fourth principle mentioned in the last chapter is evident once more, namely that the best thing we can do for our partners is to tend to our own individuation. Then relationship is not burdened by so much impossible projection.

Taking Care of the Caretaking Business

Becky was a thirty-five-year-old social worker who arrived at her career the usual way, by being a parentified child, obliged at an early age to seek to heal the parent, in the wistful hope that then the parent would be there to act as a parent should. Fate allotted her a weak, emotionally stunted mother and a narcissistic, unavailable father. When he left for the West Coast singing "California Dreaming," she became mother to her mother.

Later, when Becky came out as a gay, neither parent reacted, for neither had been involved in her journey anyway. Sadly, the history of Becky's relationships replicated her experience of those Primal Others. She was drawn to emotionally needy women who wanted a caretaker, as her mother had, or narcissistic women who were demanding but never generous in turn. As Becky had learned the heroine's role well, she could carry both styles of relationship, working two jobs, paying the bills, yet always feeling sad and a bit puzzled. Though she seemed to thrive, the lost, abandoned little girl was always just beneath the surface.

Her crisis time came when her dad, burned out in California, decided to return to the East Coast and retire. Becky knew what that meant: he would expect her to replace the women he had always managed to find to serve his neediness. While none had stayed permanently, there had been no dearth of applicants for the job. On the one hand she was enraged that this man who had left her years before would casually return and expect her to be there for him, but she also felt overwhelmed with anxiety at setting limits, creating boundaries, saying "no." She was articulate enough when she explained her need for her own life to her father and mother, but when the former declared himself "hurt and misunderstood," and the latter was forlorn, her resolve collapsed.

As we often see, the conscious clarity of the adult is overrun by the angst activated in an encounter with the Primal Others. This regressive activation of energy contaminates all adult relationships. It is especially powerful when one is obliged to deal with one's actual parents because the imago of the past is reinforced a thousandfold by the physical presence of the Primal Other.

Becky's dilemma is common to us all—how do we accurately evaluate our options and make purposeful decisions when we are so powerfully influenced by our past? Our capacity to be here, now, is always highly problematic. On paper the choice seems clear; in the therapeutic hour the choice seems clear. But holding on to consciousness when history floods us is one of the most difficult things we ever do. And achieving it now is no guarantee that we can do the same tomorrow. Only the sustained effort to remain conscious simultaneously of our own unique journey and the earlier, blocking paradigm, brings the possibility of mature choice.

At this writing Becky nervously awaits her father's return. Either she will be able firmly to define her boundaries, possibly unleashing an emotional Armageddon, or lose herself for the sake of Mom and Dad.

The Lonely Paladin

Nathan was a forty-four-year-old businessman, highly successful in his professional life. When he came into therapy, he, like Gregory, was seeing three different women, as well as shepherding his son through college and attending to his former wife. The three current, intimate relationships seemed sensible to him, and he had been clear with each partner about not wanting to commit.

Paradoxically, the crisis for Nathan arose when he was presented with a major career choice. He was enticed to leave the number two company in his field for a senior position with its major competitor. While the choice seemed clear, based on the salary and the greater opportunities, Nathan found himself quite anxious and blocked. Finally, in therapy, it became clear to him that what he was really afraid of was the commitment demanded by the new position. While it would give him more, it would also ask much more of him, and for several years to come.

Thus, the invitation to commitment had once again raised its troublesome head. Nathan wished to be entirely ethical in his dealings with partners and with his new company, but he also felt undermined by an angst which seemed unrelated to the overt tasks of the new position. This internal conflict produced an agonizing delay in making the choice.

When we recall that the psyche is logical, always logical, though serving a logos which may be other than that of ego's agenda, we can see that the fear of commitment is the fear of an engulfing closeness. The child is not born with this fear; quite the contrary, it yearns for closeness and reassurance. Fearing commitment is fearing too much closeness, and one would only have such fear if one had felt overwhelmed before, especially at a time when one felt powerless to establish boundaries.

I asked Nathan what he thought he feared. He answered quite openly that he feared domination by the Other, that he would lose track of himself in the relationship; both career and marriage would strip him of the diversity of his life, his geographic and emotional mobility, and everything would become routine and boring.

That last fear brings to mind Marie-Louise von Franz's classic delineation of the psychology of the *puer aeternus,* or eternal child, for whom the new is always tremendously exciting and the known unutterably boring.[58] Such an attitude is a convenient rationale for skipping out and onward to the next fascinating person or opportunity, which, unencumbered by history, remains pristine until it, too, devolves into the known.

As Nathan described these emotions I pushed him further. "What fears lie beneath those fears? You are a strong person. You could handle the fears you have already identified." Then Nathan felt deeply stirred and expressed emotion-laden thoughts which seemed to come from another place in the mind. "Life is not safe," he said. "People are not what they appear to be."

When asked where this came from, he hearkened back to his family's struggle against poverty and the difficulties of survival in the new land. He felt that they never talked about the realities that beset them, nor did they welcome feelings. As is true with many immigrant families, or those sorely pressed economically, such expression of emotion would have been considered a luxury. But their lack of emotional expressivity was interpreted by the child Nathan that he could not know them for who they were, even as he felt he was not sought or known by them. Thus trust in those Others was profoundly damaged.

---

[58] See *Puer Aeternus: A Psychological Study of the Adult Struggle with the Paradise of Childhood.*

As a child Nathan often thought, "I am not them." He did not know who he was, but he knew that who he intuited himself to be was someone other than who was reflected so dimly back to him. Thus his personal mythos was born—the self-sufficient hero who in another era would have been a knight-errant, a paladin who would travel on from flag to flag and not let the clinging moss grow under him. His professional success was an obvious compensation for the struggles of his family. His marriage had been early, hasty and dictated by custom. His current style of holding commitment at arm's length served to protect him not only from entrapment, but from further being hurt by the betrayal of the Other, who would never be as promised.

From this core set-up, the imago of an entrapping, betraying, disappointing Other, his strategies to avoid further wounding make logical sense. Only the conflict he felt between the new job offer, with its obvious benefits, and his angst-ridden ambivalence about it, brought this psycho-logic into conscious view. As one can surmise, the capacity to make the wound conscious, and all the psychological strategies which flow therefrom, require that we consciously suffer the angst these dynamics embody. The grown-up Nathan cannot evade this pain, but as an adult capable of understanding its infantile origins, he can take a stand where the child could not. As an adult he deserves a relationship and a challenging career as much as the next person. His capacity to make conscious the imago which derives from another time, another place, gives him the chance to be in the here and now, and then to make choices that serve the adult's desire for life rather than the child's originally necessary but now self-defeating defenses.

Fate had a trick in store for Nathan. As he wrestled with the new job offer, he realized that what attracted him was only the money and perks. But, in dealing with the problem of commitment to that job, he had unearthed the secret fear which all commitment obliges. Then, when the one woman of the three for whom he really cared decided to move to a distant city, Nathan realized not only that he loved her, but that what had kept him at bay was his fear. At this writing he is seriously considering moving to that same city to be with her, and operating his business from there. Quite a revolution.

Nathan had broken through the constrictions occasioned by his family of origin. In the end, the question was not about this job or that, this partner or that, but whether he had the wherewithal to grow up. From that breakthrough the rest is relatively easy.

Necessary Questions

Implicit in the task of becoming conscious of wounded eros are certain questions which constitute an inventory of self and Other. If we do not ask them of ourselves, then our partners will, or we will hit some wall which obliges us to begin. Among them are:

1. Where do my dependencies show up in the relationship?

2. What am I asking my partner to do for me that I, as a mature adult, need to be doing for myself?

3. How do I repeatedly constrict myself through my historically conditioned attitudes and behavior patterns?

4. Am I taking too much responsibility for the emotional well-being of the Other? Am I taking on his or her journey at the expense of my own, and if so, why?

5. Am I living my life in such a fashion that I will be happy with the consequences of my choices? If not, when do I plan to start? What fears, lack of permission or old behaviors block me from living my life?

6. In what ways do I seek to avoid suffering?[59]

Such questions reach down and into our souls. They stir old wounds, test our defenses and illuminate the strategies we play out with our partners. Finally, they reveal not only why our relationships are wounded, but also ways in which we can heal them by first healing ourselves.

Of course, it is impossible to avoid the wounding of eros. One must acknowledge, too, that in many lives such wounds have been

---

[59] See my *Swamplands of the Soul: New Life in Dismal Places* for a fuller discussion of the dynamic relationship between suffering and growth.

the spur to great acts of creativity, or the sublimation of nature's desires on behalf of service to the culture. Historically, the advance of civilization has depended on the expression of eros in multitudinous ways: four centuries to build a cathedral, soldiers willing to die for an abstraction, and many, many daily sacrifices of self on behalf of conventional mores. But in every case, the wound is to the individual soul. How many have lived their whole lives shrouded in guilt and repression for the merest manifestation of the natural desires of their own soul? How many have been punished, even martyred, for following the summons to their own destiny?

We may solemnly mourn all those who have been destroyed by repressive ideologies, insecure institutions, fearful leaders. We may grieve the loss of so much capacity for love, so much individual potential, slain by the weight of the collective. But in the end, we, too, are required to pursue our own path toward wholeness. We carry forever the original woundings of eros, but as adults we are responsible for those wounds, responsible for making them conscious, healing them, and thereby freeing ourselves and others from our pathology.

5
Eros in Organizations

All of life is relational. As we have seen, the quality of our relationships to others is a direct function of the relationship we have evolved with ourselves, which in turn has generally resulted from the internalization of our relationships with the Primal Others.

So, we are forever transferring the dynamics of another time, another place, to this moment, this relationship. And others are transferring their psychological history to us. Thus we are never free of relationship dynamics, even when alone. Of course, much of our lives is not spent alone; most of us spend over half of our waking hours relating to collective structures of family, work and institutional life. It is important, therefore, in addition to our reflections on the character of intimate relationship, to consider the dynamics of collective life as well.

Sociologists make a clear distinction between *society* and *community*. A society is a group of persons organized to serve a set of purposes, some short term, some long term. The plane ride with strangers is a temporary society whose purpose or motive is to move from one place to another. Along the way we may sleep, stare out the window or converse with whomever fate has placed beside us. When we arrive, each member goes a separate way and the society dissolves, never to be exactly reconstituted. Societies are thus very fragile. They survive only as long as their constituent members are committed to the same purpose. When that has been met, or the members lose interest, the society dissolves.

A community forms when the members of a society have had a common transcendent experience, one that lifts each person out of his or her isolation to participate in the transformation. Should that plane go down, for instance, the crash survivors might very well experience community, given the large event which had proved a transcendent encounter. Each person remains an individual, but each is also now identified psychologically with the transcendent experience; each is more than he or she was previously. This is the nature of tribal experience, where shared history, ancestors and mythology provide the vertical dimension that links each person in the community. Even communities, as we have seen, risk losing contact with the shared transcendent history; then they may devolve into a society which in turn lacks the power to bind its members for very long.

A notable example of the shift from community to society may be witnessed in the dissolution of the Kiowa Indian nation. Premier bison hunters, the Kiowa flourished as long as their totemic relationship with the bison, their link to the gods, survived. The prayers before and after the hunt, and the respectful employment of all parts of the beast shared by them with the gods, provided the tribe with a transcendent totemic connection. When the bison were annihilated, the linkage to the sacred was severed and the Kiowa quickly dissolved, absorbed by the encroaching Anglo culture. This is a cautionary tale, for in their experience we see what happens when a community loses its common purpose. This is evident also in mainstream cultures, where crime, social anomie, addictions and sociopathies are not-so-mute testimony to the dissolution of community. We are now a society, not a community.

Most people experience their work environment as a society, not a community, and suffer from the difference. Most places of employment are organized around the purpose of providing a product or service. The employees are not, generally speaking, identified with that product or service. A friend of mine once worked for a large food manufacturer and said he had to leave when he realized that even in their free time he and his colleagues felt obliged to talk about cookies. I hear similar stories from those who have worked for other major corporations. There is a mythos, to be sure, but no product or service feeds the soul. Organizations fueled only by such a horizontal purpose are lacking in the vertical dimension that gives one a sense of meaning, participation in something transcendent, membership in a vital community. In a word, they lack soul.

We cannot readily define "soul," but we surely experience its presence or absence. Whether we will or no, we bring the needs of the soul to the work environment and suffer its neglect. Another friend, Director of Human Resources at a large multinational corporation, gave a standard speech to new employees. His comments may seem shocking, insensitive, but his intent was in fact compassionate. "The company," he told them, "does not love you. It rents your behavior only so long as that behavior is productive and makes money for the corporation." His speech was designed to make employees more conscious of their own legitimate needs and the fact that those needs would not be met by the corporation. They needed to tend to their personal lives, to cultivate their intimate relationships, and be very clear about what the company would provide (an income) and what it would not (love).

Whoever loses contact with his or her own soul is in trouble. Similarly, organizations that pay no attention to matters of soul are in trouble, even when financially productive. The current practices of so-called downsizing, managed care and bottom-line thinking in business and academe have led to the effacement of soul and the erosion of morale. Downsizing is a euphemism for depriving people of their livelihood. Managed care is really managed cost, a service only to insurance companies. Bottom-line thinking is too often thinking with your head in your bottom.

The American Medical Association long ago won its battle against socialized medicine, but then lost it to corporate capitalism. Every physician, psychologist and social worker I know reports that his or her professional judgment and treatment plan has been interfered with by insurance companies, with an accompanying loss of professional and personal morale as well as quality of treatment.

The world of academe, long before big business, saw the advantage of using students as underpaid, part-time assistants to whom no benefits or security are offered. Anyone who has spent much time on college campuses knows that professors are growing increasingly paranoid, cynical and disaffected. The love of their subject matter that brought them to teaching in the first place is being overburdened by political and administrative considerations. So the direct relationship between students and teachers has become eroded and lifeless, without eros. With eros, learning is infectious. Without eros, students feel despised and cease to care about the subject itself, motivated only by marks. In both business and academia (if there is still a difference), morale is low, suspicion and cynicism high. Institutions are no longer communities; they have become fragile societies with little grounding in transcendent values.

Corporations of even modest size now employ specialists in what is called Organizational Development. Their work is to mobilize and direct employees' energies, in the most humane fashion possible, toward the achievement of corporate goals. As individuals, we too have goals and are similarly invested in the management of our energy. When our energies are directed toward goals consonant with the soul's intention, then we feel a sense of well-being. When libido is directed toward ends dissonant with the soul's teleology, then we become neurotic. By analogy, those organizations whose management of energy does not serve their true purpose will also suffer a splitting, a corporate neurosis as it were.

At the risk of straining the analogy between individual and corporation, let us pursue it provisionally. Organizations are both the sum of the individuals that comprise them and something more than the sum of their parts. Corporations also embody a synergy which, as in interpersonal relationships, can achieve no higher level of development than the contribution individuals are able to make. To the extent that we are neurotic as individuals, so our corporate life will similarly suffer the transference of those dynamics.

In *The Psychopathology of Everyday Life,* Freud argued that one does not have to visit a psychiatric hospital to observe psychopathology. One can see it in ordinary folks in ordinary settings— through forgetting, slips of the tongue and the like—everyday events that intimate extraordinary dynamics in the tenebrous conflict of id, ego and superego. Later, Jung demonstrated the existence of complexes which function autonomously in us all. Activation of these charged clusters of energy transfers the experiences of other times and places to the present, undermining our capacity for conscious choice and holding us hostage to the past.

All relationships are contaminated by unconscious material, especially so when complexes have been activated. Intimate relationships naturally evoke our primal complexes because intimacy comes closest to the analogue with the original parental relationships. But organizations also receive the transferred power of these complexes. Mostly commonly activated in organizations are the parental and authority complexes. Just as the child, impressed by the inequity of power between child and parent, makes its strategic adaptations, so the individual in corporate life transfers the stratagems of history to the present. As we know, nature provides us with the either/or choice of fight or flight. In the extreme, the fight stratagem leads employees to aggression and sabotage, while flight leads to passive-aggressive behavior—sloth and avoidance of duty, substance abuse, absenteeism.

Similarly, the projection of parental authority onto an employer causes us to expect that the company will love us, give us security, meet our emotional needs. Fat chance! But it is always shocking when one is "down-sized," for one was unconsciously expecting the corporate Other to be "the good breast." Having experienced the powerlessness and dependency of childhood, it is natural to project onto the corporate Other the power, wisdom and nurturant intent we once expected from the parent. That such a feeling state continues to exist in the face of experiential reality is a measure of its power.

Internalized childhood experience not only influences our one-on-one relationships, it is also transferred to our experience of organizations. From having felt engulfed, we learn to placate the powerful Other. In its most extreme form, this behavior is called co-dependence, where one's own reality and well-being are sacrificed in service to the Other. In corporate life this produces the compliant employee, not the one who will risk telling the truth to a superior, or risk initiative in service of corporate development. Such power inequities produce avoidant behaviors in many forms which, again, do not serve the well-being of the corporation whose health depends on the best contributions the individual can make. Alternatively, those who suffered the early wound of abandonment, with the attendant lack of self-esteem, are likewise inhibited in contributing to corporate goals. Driven by the need for reassurance by the Other, such persons will be inclined to seek praise, to toady up to superiors.

All employees bring a measure of anxiety to corporate relationships. Some will be unable to bring their best energies to corporate life, nor will their morale be high. Gregory, discussed in the last chapter, once observed that the secret of his corporate leadership was his capacity to make employees feel better about themselves in the context of their work life. Even those he had to fire, he said, remained friendly because their sense of self had been enhanced rather than diminished.

When we recall that the provisional personality is an assemblage of behaviors, attitudes toward self and Other, and reflexive strategies designed to manage the anxieties of childhood, we see how corporate life can bear the imprint of the past. No wonder corporations sometimes seem stuck. Corporations activate the analogues of primordial relationships; they replicate the family of origin dynamics and reevoke the authority complex. For these reasons collective life is frequently infantilizing and injurious. Religious institutions prevent people from transformative experience; schools teach children to distrust learning; governments oppress those they were formed to serve; hospitals make patients sick; and corporations wonder why their employees are not loyal. The more the false self is activated, the more history intrudes upon the present, the more the collective atmosphere is contaminated.

Many organizations arise from some noble idea or compelling purpose, but over time their underlying values may be forgotten or become outmoded. Then the highest priorities become to ensure their survival and to protect their priesthood. The corporation may defile its founding values, make brutal decisions based on abstract notions of corporate interest rather than the well-being of its citizenry. Priests promote the notion that they are indispensable, professors that they are a necessary elite, and corporate managers frontload their perks and backload their golden parachutes.

Institutions, then, can not only lose their soul but can become demonic. Even a good idea becomes demonic when it becomes one-sided, exclusive and resistant to dialogue.

As an institution is the sum of its individuals, and more, so it is also a reflection of its leadership. Where the leader is stuck psychologically, the corporation too will be stuck. How can the Church foster spiritual life when its pastors are unconscious of their own shadows? How can a company win the trust of its public and its employees when it lives a lie? How can educators illuminate when they cannot shed light on their own darkness? As Jung wrote:

> Every educator . . . should constantly ask himself whether he is actually fulfilling his teachings in his own person and in his own life, to the best of his knowledge and with a clear conscience. Psychotherapy has taught us that in the final reckoning it is not knowledge, not technical skill, that has a curative effect, but the personality of the doctor. And it is the same with education: it presupposes self-education.[60]

Just as Jung observed that the greatest burden the child must bear is the unconscious life of the parent, so it might be said that the secret psychic burden of any institution will be an expression of where its leadership is blocked on a personal level. The contamination of corporate life may not seem as visible as a personal neurosis, but it filters into all levels nonetheless.

In *The Republic,* Plato asks who is fit to rule. He was not a democrat; he argued for "the philosopher-king," which we might translate today as "the psychologically integrated leader." Such a person, were he or she available, would bring depth and the enlightened (that is conscious) use of power. As we know, those who seek power over others often do so only to compensate for their insecurity. Those who need a badge and a gun to feel empowered are unworthy of the trust of the public. Those who lust for public

---

[60] "The Gifted Child," *The Development of Personality,* CW 17, par. 240.

office are unfit for it. Those who need power are caught in complexes and in the end everyone around them will suffer. In the United States we have come a long way from the time of talented citizens like Washington, Franklin and Jefferson, who were drafted into positions of political authority by the request of their comrades and their high sense of public duty. Today we see professional politicians who faint not at the thought of changing their values to accord with opinion polls, and whose chief motivation is not public service but personal fame.

The style of the organization inevitably filters down from the executive suite. The small man with the Napoleonic complex, the gaming magnate who names casinos after herself, the leader whose name and picture dominate the front page of the in-house organ, are all prototypes of personal neurosis as corporate pathology.

I once worked with two professional finance executives who labored for a family-owned, mid-size business in the entertainment sector. The family pathology nearly drove the company to bankruptcy many times, and certainly drove the two financial guys into therapy. Family members were driven by greed, narcissism and immaturity. They constantly milked the corporation of its liquid assets. They loved to flaunt their wealth, even maintaining an expensive corporate plane. Their immaturity was characterized by lack of personal discipline, poor attention span, desire for instant gratification; they were easily distracted and paid no attention to the effect of their behavior on their employees. My two clients, separately and jointly responsible for keeping the company afloat, had to bail the family out several times.

How treatable is such a situation? Get another job! Any therapist will report that a client with poor discipline, poor attention span, a desire for instant gratification and an irresponsible attitude toward the consequences of his or her acts will not enter therapy, or if there by happenstance, will not work at it. Such persons create sick companies and sick employees. And they will not change, even if the banks close their gates some day. There is a time to treat a condition, and there is a time to leave it. Both of the men I knew had been made ill by the conditions in which they worked and the impossible expectations under which they had to operate. Both decided to save themselves rather than continue to suffer the consequences of someone else's unexamined life.

On the other hand, I saw the head of a manufacturing corporation who was the third generation to inherit the responsibility. When his father retired, Edward was summoned from another part of the country, and from a job he loved, to assume responsibility not only for the corporation but for the extended family whose income depended on the health of the factory. So great was the familial expectation, including that of his own wife, that Edward felt he had to make this necessary sacrifice of his own vocation. He came to therapy depressed, without knowing why. It was soon clear that his depression derived from the suppression of his own calling. This conflict was carried very deeply in him and all his dreams seemed to point to the price of losing contact with his personal vocation.

After a few months of repetitive messages in his dreams, Edward came to believe in their truth. He felt that he still needed to support the extended family, but he also needed to carry the split more consciously. At this writing Edward has a realistic five-year plan which will bring the company to a certain plateau where the family will be well provided for, and he can honorably leave. He has hired a manager of daily operations, freeing himself for long-term strategy and private projects. He has redecorated his offices to make them more aesthetically satisfying, and rented a private space where he goes to play music, write and read what he wants. His family knows of this retreat but none is allowed to encroach. This is how Edward is taking care of both his soul and his collective responsibilities. And the company, meanwhile, is flourishing as never before.

Most organizations ignore issues pertaining to the quality of life of their employees. Such considerations would seem to most managers to be superfluous, costly indulgences. But workers spend half their waking lives in that atmosphere, which surely affects morale, and morale clearly affects productivity. True bottom-line thinking would give greater attention to quality of life issues.

I once taught at a college whose architecture won a national award. It was a series of gray, linear corridors with steel and glass structures and interchangeable walls. While it was certainly functional, and created an interesting contrast with the surrounding forest, the effect of the building itself worked against education. The structure promoted uniformity, mobility, interchangeability and a steady flow of units. These are the values which best serve an airport, not a college where grounding, centering and connectedness are intricately bound up with the educational mission. There was a large airfield nearby, and I had the fantasy that one day a 747 would land in the parking lot and those linear corridors would suddenly fill with passengers looking for the baggage claim section.

For those who spend years in such structures, the cumulative effect is dullness and depression. To three separate presidents of this college I suggested that the mere addition of different colors of paint to the gray walls would bring greater warmth to classrooms and corridors. They probably thought me mad, and surely thought the cost unwarranted. What we had at that college was a society, consciously devoted to a task, but we never had community.

While it is true that the role of organizations and universities is not to play Mother, there is something seriously amiss when those at the top do not realize that their own survival depends to some extent on the well-being of those in their charge. Employee Assistance programs are a good sign, assuming complete confidentiality and nonpunitive consequences for those who seek help. They are certainly cheaper in the long run than the sum of lost working days due to stress, mental illness and substance abuse. Similarly, it is well known that mood and morale are affected by color, sound, scent and texture, therefore it is only common sense to pay attention to such influences when designing places to work.

Communication styles also have a substantial impact on corporate relationships. Attentive interest in employee opinion and suggestions contribute greatly to morale and a sense of joint commitment. One man who took over an educational institution spent the first days in personal interviews with key employees. He sought to learn who they were, about their families, their interests and what they were most able to contribute. He told them they probably knew what worked and what didn't better than he did, and he wanted their most candid input. This consultation process brought him much vital information, helpful suggestions and staff enthusiasm. It all seems so obvious, but how many of us have been treated in a similar way in our working life?

Corporate morale is also noticeably improved when people are encouraged to have a personal vision and to share their proposals with supervisors who will take them seriously. Many years ago, when my father worked on a factory assembly line, he figured out an incentive plan that would increase both productivity and morale. Union and management agreed that these twin goals were achievable by his plan, but vetoed it anyway rather than change to something unfamiliar. As they could not foresee, and control, possible consequences, they stayed locked in the old paradigm which served the psychological health of neither the company nor its employees. (Sounds like the Abilene paradox again—everyone agrees, and then does the opposite.)

If we push the analogy of personal and corporate relationships a bit further, we might conclude that the healing of corporate life ought to be pursued in a fashion similar to that by which we seek personal healing. Jung suggested that neurosis is symptomatic of a reduced vision of life, a world-view of insufficient amplitude. For the individual to heal, he or she must recover a better relationship to soul. For corporate bodies to heal, they must have managers who will address the question of soul. And we cannot expect them to do this for their companies if they have not done it for themselves. As Jung repeatedly warned, the therapist cannot accompany the patient any further than the therapist has gone. Therefore, the willingness to address one's personal healing is essential before one can contribute a measure of healing to the collective.

Admittedly, this is asking a lot of corporate culture, where profit and loss are quantifiable, where pleasing shareholders is paramount and where hanging on to one's job by offending no one is acceptable. But, as Plato noted in *The Republic,* the relationship between the health of the ruler and that of the land is inescapable.

Both individually and as a manager, each of us must enquire into the matter of the personal shadow. "What in myself can I not face, and where does that leak out? What complexes drive me? What does power over others mean to me? For what insecurities am I compensating?" These are tough questions for anyone, especially for those whose chief training has been to manage externals and hide what is inside. Such considerations are heroic and revolutionary, and, when undertaken seriously, change the corporate ambience in amazing ways. The energies that emanate from us affect others, sometimes infect them, and always influence them. To the extent that our personal energies are healthy, the world around us may be able to change for the better. This is as true in our working environment as it is in our intimate relationships.

Can we expect to psychoanalyze corporate life when such enquiry is difficult even at the individual level? Perhaps not, but it is at least urgent to raise the level of consciousness in organizations, to address matters of soul in places where such questions have been neglected to the detriment of all. Even much of the healing profession has become dominated by economic values rather than by care of the soul. Think about it. How many therapists in North America identify themselves as primarily psychodynamic, meaning depth oriented, concerned with the interface between conscious and unconscious? To my knowledge, very few, perhaps ten percent. The others practice behavioral modification, cognitive restructuring and psychopharmacology. Each of these has a legitimate contribution to make, but they all neglect the question that most troubles us—the question of meaning. As Jung noted, sometimes "the clinical practice of psychotherapy is a mere makeshift that does its utmost to prevent numinous experiences."[61]

The search for meaning is a quintessentially human characteristic. To ignore it is tragic. When we recall that the Greek word for

---

[61] *Letters,* vol. 2, p. 118.

soul is *psyche,* then we are struck by the absurd paradox that most of modern psychology has lost contact with the psyche.

The treatment of soul is what heals, finally, whether at the individual or the corporate level. This means disciplining the ego to ask, patiently and sincerely, "What does the soul ask of me?" And then to serve that purpose to the best of one's abilities. Most of modern psychology has lost its nerve in the face of the large and demanding questions of soul, and thus has narrowed and often trivialized its mission. Modern organizational life too seldom addresses questions of soul. Faced with the power of quarterly reports, soul is forgotten and the real bottom line always shows a loss.

All of us, at all levels of collective participation, need to recover our nerve, to find the will and courage to ask more about meaning, to oppose depersonalization, to again stand up for soul. Jung once observed that life "is a short episode between two great mysteries."[62] Our task, on both the personal and the corporate level, is to make sure we don't squander our energies in this in-between time. The task starts at home, but we must also carry it on into the world.

---

[62] Ibid., vol. 1, p. 483.

6

The Spindrift Gaze Toward Paradise

Bind us in time, O Seasons clear, and awe.
O minstrel galleons of Carib fire,
Bequeath us to no earthly shore until
Is answered in the vortex of our grave
The seal's wide spindrift gaze toward paradise.
—Hart Crane, "Voyages."

As we have seen, the programming of the imago of the Other derives essentially from the child's phenomenological experience of primal relationships. That imago is always present, in both intimate and collective relationships. Would it not be reasonable, then, to assume that such programming is present also in our search for relationship with the Absolute Other, traditionally called God?

Here we enter dangerous waters. Those who are part of a particular faith tradition will insist on the existence of an Absolute Other, with its own independent qualities which may be perceived "through a glass, darkly" (1 Cor. 13:12), or in the revelatory events of history, or embodied in sacred texts. Although the religious attitudes of most are merely received, that is, derivative of tribe or tradition, for some individuals faith assertions are irrefutable because they are immediate, immanent and experiential. While one may enlarge one's sensibility through the encounter with the reality of another (which is the chief service of relationship), one seldom makes headway challenging the reality another has experienced. That such "realities" are often fringed with, and protected by, complexes, makes them even more susceptible to dogmatic defense.

It is generally known that Freud was hostile to the idea of religious experience. He tips his hand even in the title of his major work on the subject, *The Future of an Illusion.* For Freud religions arise out of our existential need to assert our autonomy over hostile na-

114

ture. Civilization, he noted, depends upon the renunciation of instinct in service to abstract goals such as collective security. These twin goals—the creation of the "illusion" of security in an insecure world, and the establishment of such abstractions as "duty," "sacrifice" and "service to the tribe"—control and channel the narcissistic character of instinctual gratification. Freud concluded that "the principal task of civilization, its actual *raison d'être,* is to defend us against nature."[63]

Thus Freud concurs with Voltaire's assertion that if God did not exist, we would have to invent him. But what kind of God? Here Freud avers that our infantile experience of the personal parent is transferred onto the cosmos. Freud thus places us on familiar ground, for we have seen how in other intimate relationships we transfer the imago of our parental experience, with its attendant dynamics, onto the Other. Freud considers this transference illusory, in that "what is characteristic of illusions is that they are derived from human wishes. In this sense they come close to psychiatric delusions."[64] As a wish-fulfillment, then, the idea of God is emotionally compelling and does not require external verification.

But where Freud is hoisted by his own petard is in thinking that his methodology itself is free of illusion. Part of *his* illusion is that "scientific work is the only road which leads us to a knowledge of reality outside ourselves."[65] He ignores the reality of *gnosis,* the immediate, unmediated, phenomenological experience which we may find, for example, through art, intellectual structures, mystical experience and the like. He relegates religious assertions to the realm of the child's fantasies of the perfect parent—all wise, protective and nurturing. At the same time, our infantile fears of incurring the disfavor of the Other, or our secret resentment of their power over us, may evoke feelings of guilt.

Freud believed that the dynamics of our early relationships,

---

[63] *The Future of an Illusion,* p. 15.
[64] Ibid., p. 3.
[65] Ibid.

when transferred to the cosmos, infantilizes. "Religion would thus be the universal obsessional neurosis of humanity."[66] As an obsession—that is, an unwanted but urgent thought—religion aborts personal growth and keeps the individual, and the society, mired in the regressive perspectives of childhood. Humankind, Freud argued, needs to be courageous enough to relinquish its dependence on the Sky Parent, grow up and face the universe nakedly, embracing an illusion-free reality.

Religious practices themselves may be judged either progressive or regressive by virtue of how they play out in a person's life. If they enlarge one's vision, support one's psychosocial development, and provide meaningful linkages to the cosmos and one's community, then surely religion is psychologically healthy. If, on the other hand, religious attitudes foster guilt, dependency, polarized thinking, shadow projections and so on, thwarting the acceptance of personal responsibility, then surely they are unhealthy.

We must admit that much of what Freud claims is valid. Religious beliefs have been responsible for myriad pogroms and massacres, for keeping people ignorant and enslaved, and for rationalizing injustice and bigotry. Moreover, we know that all things which emanate from the human bear the mark of the human, that we cannot help but anthropomorphize the unknowable. What we say about God is finally saying more about ourselves than the mystery we call God. Also, we can see infantile attitudes in many theological assertions. It is not a crime to wish for the perfect parent, but it may be, as Freud argued, an illusion to impose that wish on the autonomous cosmos in order to assuage our anxieties.

However, Freud tends to throw out the whole experience of the transcendent on the basis that much of what issues from humanity is generated by infantile experience. Freud was passionate about this issue, suggesting an active complex of his own. He certainly rebelled against his family's rabbinical past, and he was caught up in the materialist, positivist Zeitgeist of late nineteenth-century

---

[66] Ibid., p. 43.

Europe. Nonetheless, it behooves any of us to exam our views and discern the infantile wishes therein. We will find them as surely in our theologies as we have found them in our intimate and corporate relationships. If we can muster the moral and intellectual courage to face those infantilizing ideas in earthly relationships, it is no less required that we trace them in our assumptions about the absolute as well. Freud is partly right, but only partly.

For Jung, on the other hand, the religious impulse is neither infantile nor a wish-fulfillment. He considered our religious longing to be as instinctual as our desire for food. "Religion," he wrote, "is an *instinctive* attitude peculiar to man, and its manifestations can be followed all through human history."[67] It arises out of the evolutionary development of our species and is most clearly the embodiment of our search for meaning. Our religiosity is of course not limited to matters of institution or creed, but is involved wheresoever we encounter depth. The theologian Paul Tillich asserted that our religion will be found wherever our "ultimate concern" is found;[68] thus for some the pursuit of power and wealth constitutes their religion, while for others it may be the longing for security. Obviously, not all expressions of religiosity will promote transcendence, but they do focus one's psychic energy in service to a value for which the ego longs.

Accordingly, we can encounter the religious in our engagement with the Other, as every lover will attest. Or we may find the religious motive operating in the unconscious and projected onto cultural artifacts. For example, some time ago I took my visiting father to an Atlantic City casino as a sort of anthropological project. He won 320 quarters. Around us were thousands of other souls, worshiping at such shrines as attract far more annual visitors (about 35,000,000 each year in the 1990s) than even New York City or Disneyworld. Their migration is religious in character, albeit essentially unconscious. They seek connection with the Other (recall the

---

[67] "The Undiscovered Self," *Civilization in Transition,* CW 10, par. 512.
[68] *Dynamics of Faith,* p. 16.

etymology of "religion," to re-connect with), transcendence of the ordinary (to be lifted out of the quotidian horizontal onto the vertical plane), and transformation (the experience of enlargement).

Certainly the longing for connection, transcendence and transformation are deeply religious urges. That they are not in the end satisfiable by money is always discovered in a short time by these modern pilgrims, though the illusion is sufficiently powerful that many return again and again.

In a quite different theater of public activity, these lines are written on the day of the funeral of Diana Spencer, images of which are being transmitted into homes all over the world. The solemnity of the occasion and the extraordinary outpouring of public emotion, as well as the sense of mutual, unifying and transcendent experience, has not been present in the United Kingdom since the Luftwaffe drummed overhead in the 1940s. Such a mass feeling must be noted not only as a sociopolitical event, but as a movement of soul and the expression of enormous psychic energy. Since few of us watching these images knew the former Princess of Wales personally, much of what we experience of her must be projected from our own psyches, dramatizing archetypal mythologems of which we have little conscious awareness. Many remember her tortured journey through marital betrayal, her descent into addictions and an eating disorder, even as many others identify with her public espousal of sympathy for the disadvantaged. All of us are stirred to project our own wounds and hopes onto this distant charismatic figure who seems to have genuinely moved those who met her.

Underneath the public drama, of course, is a vast shift of populist sensibility. The attitudes which once served an empire, and continue in establishment circles, seem now out of touch not only with the disenfranchised but also with modern Euro-unity, cyberspace and the global community. As one television commentator put it bluntly, "The people are tired of toffs in tweed, who don't have to face election, hunting grouse in Scotland." (The recent change of governing parties, and the "loss" of Hong Kong, are other indices of this sea-change in the social structure and assumptions). Diana, then, typified an emergent sensibility, and the expression of affection and grief at her funeral constitute the people's referendum on England's future.

But in the shock, denial and dismay of this past week, similar to what many of us experienced at the assassination of John F. Kennedy, something even more primal is afoot, something that pulls on our deepest assumptions about the cosmos. Why someone like a Diana would become such a cynosure of public scrutiny and curiosity in the first place, to the point of paparazzi seeking to satiate our private hungers, is the deeper question. And it is a question about us. That we do not, as a civilization, ask such a question is what helped harry and devour her.

In the enormity of the projections onto a figure like Diana, or other culture icons like Elvis, we see much of our own dynamics. As Karl Jaspers and Paul Tillich asked, we are obliged to "read" the artifacts of our culture in order to discern the movement of soul beneath.[69] In the dismay following her death, we observe not only the natural shock of unexpected trauma, but a profound disbelief, as if thousands of others were not dying at the same moment in twisted wreckages of one sort or another.

It is in this disbelief that we find our own deep fantasy that, somehow, there are magical beings. If there are magical beings, special, transcendent, exempt, then there is hope for us. But the car wreck in a Parisian tunnel dislodges this assumption—none of us is special, transcendent, exempt. Death is the great leveler, and there are no exceptions. Of course we all know this, rationally, but in our heart of hearts we still hope for the Magical Other. If there are really magical beings, then magic may save us. If there is no magic,

---

[69] Elvis Presley now has religious denominations based upon him, with attendant miracles, pilgrimages of the faithful, sacred relics and petitionary prayers. Strange as that may seem, who would have thought a disgraced, crucified malefactor, his followers in flight, would have formed the psychic nexus for a two-thousand-year-old religion? Who would have expected an itinerant, ill-educated corporal from Austria to have fashioned anything out of the rummage of misfits who formed the original German Worker's Party, something called NASDAP?

whether from sacred institutions or special beings, then we are all lost—or so we fear.

This feeling is hardly new. We see it with archetypal clarity in the dilemma of Job. He was a pious man who lived by the rules and by his assumed assurance of a contract with the Cosmic Other. He behaved on his side of the ledger, therefore the universe should also behave. Perhaps Yahweh found this assumption resonant of the good child whose naivete needs enlargement. Job learns there is no contract. For all the loss of family, property and creature comfort, the greatest shock comes from his loss of the presumed contract. Like all of us, Job wanted a special deal; he wanted magic. Yet out of his unwanted, undeserved suffering, a larger being emerges. He moves from the obedient, pious child who behaves as expected to a man who has had a genuine encounter with the numinous. "I have heard of Thee by the hearing of the ear," he says to Yahweh, "but now mine eye seeth thee." (Job 42:5) Job's search for the Magical Other is our search, and his end is ours.

What is most deeply psychological here is also deeply religious. We seek to pawn off the difficulty of our journey onto the Other. Part of our task in clearing that up has to do with growing up, as Job did, and facing the cosmos unaided by the Magical Other.

During this week I could not help but think of Diana's country-man, Thomas Nashe. His Job-like democratizing lesson in 1792 derived from the Great Plague which was then sweeping England. King and commoner, cleric and magistrate, peasant and burgher— all were at the mercy of that invisible power which erupted in black buboes on their lymph glands and painfully took them within forty-eight hours. In "A Litany in Time of Plague," Nashe invokes the lesson all of us learn, or relearn, in time. In evoking the fabled beauty of Troy, he reminds us not only of Diana, but of ourselves.

> Brightness falls from the air;
> Queens have died young and fair;
> Dust hath closed Helen's eye.[70]

---

[70] *Norton Anthology of Poetry*, p. 202.

As natural phenomena, then, cultural expressions of soul are as worthy of analysis as are our dreams and complexes. Similarly, we are obliged to analyze what psychic stratagems may be afoot in overtly religious phenomena. Jung asserted that "the term 'religion' designates the attitude peculiar to a consciousness which has been changed by experience of the *numinosum*."[71] He exasperated many theologians by refusing to identify the origin of the *numinosum,* whether within us or "out there." That, he said, is a matter of metaphysical speculation and/or personal faith. His province was the examination of what occurs in the human psyche, and is therefore experiential.

Paradoxically, Jung's refusal to make the metaphysical leap was a way in which he honored the mystery of the Mystery. Recall the etymology of the word "numinous," suggesting the verb "to wink." It is as if whatever lies in our depths winks at us and we are obliged to respond. That winking activates an archetypal structure within us which then shapes an inner energy into what Jung called the "god-imago." (It is the function of the archetype to provide not content but intent, not to provide meaning, as such, but to direct libido toward that gestalt which is experienced as meaningful.)

Note that Jung does not say the imago *is* God, rather that the imago is our experience of the numinous in the post-Kantian epoch. Such reverence for the Mystery is appropriate to a religious attitude. He warned against our tendency to fall in love with our own ego artifacts, to reify and literalize our metaphors:

> God is a mystery, and everything we say about it is said and believed by human beings. We make images and concepts, and when I speak of God I always mean the image man has made of him. But no one knows what he is like, or he would be a god himself.[72]

Such a reminder of the finitude of our minds, of our theologies as so many Rorschach blots, of the anthropomorphic imprint of our psychic projections, of our deeply subjective readings of mystery

---

[71] "Psychology and Religion," *Psychology and Religion,* CW 11, par. 9.
[72] *Letters,* vol. 2, p. 384.

filtered through our cultural lenses and personal neuroses, is a fitting summons to humility.

Sadly, the history of theology from the Old Testament prophets to current televangelists is one of arrogant presumption about the Absolute Other and self-delusion. We must beware of those who talked with God this morning, got the inside track on what is right for us, and now seek to coerce our compliance with their agenda through the induction of guilt.

The internal carrier of the god-imago is what Jung called the Self. Thus the idea of God relates not just to the parent, as Freud surmised, but to our own longing for wholeness. It is not that we desire to become God, but that we desire that expression of wholeness which constitutes our own divinity. Since God remains the Absolute Other, or the Wholly Other as defined by Karl Barth, we cannot know God as such, but in our own intimations of wholeness we intuit the wholeness of the Wholly Other. The ego's role in all this is to cooperate with that balance of opposites which constitutes our encounter with truth.

Jung's most succinct definition of neurosis is that it is generated by the one-sidedness of the personality. Whatever absolute truth may be, we can only experience it through polarities, a fact pontiffs and preachers sometimes forget. The minor truths are easily contradicted. For great truths, their opposites are also true. As Jung noted, "The self is made manifest in the opposites and in the conflict between them. . . . Hence the way to the self begins with conflict."[73]

Alas, conflict is troubling to the ego, and so we have many ploys by which to stifle dissenting voices, ranging from repression and dissociation to distorting them to fit our hidden agenda. If the ego's prime need is security, then the relationship to ultimate mystery, that is, to truth as Wholly Other, is inherently problematic, for the otherness of the Other, as we have seen in the field of interpersonal relationship, is very difficult to bear. Yet it is precisely in the understanding of this internal conflict that Jung has most to offer. The

---

[73] *Psychology and Alchemy,* CW 12, par. 259.

attendance upon such conflict, whether in the area of interpersonal relationship or in our encounter with Mystery, leads us in time, if not to clarity, at least to enlargement. To the objection that many conflicts are intrinsically insoluble, Jung replied,

> People sometimes take this view because they think only of external solutions—which at bottom are not solutions at all. . . . A real solution comes only from within, and then only because the patient has been brought to a different attitude.[74]

Thus, as we saw in regard to interpersonal relationship, the prime service of the Other is to *remain* Other, not to become an artifact of our ego's colonial impulses. This may trouble the ego, but it is a prerequisite to psychological growth. As the Greek tragedians noted, it is only through suffering that we come to wisdom. No ego seeks suffering, but in every suffering occasion there is an invitation to growth—if we can bear it.

So Job, the much belabored Everyman of old, moved from a received piety to an encounter with the living, terrifying God. He did not want to know God that well. He did not want to see the world as God saw it. But the Mystery had other intentions, and Job became the prototype of all of us who say we want relationship, but in fact mean only if we remain in control. Yes, the autonomy of the Other is truly frightening, whether in intimacy or in a relationship with the cosmos.

Jung was a deeply religious soul, most of all because he cared greatly about such questions as his personal relationship to the Mystery. As a child he had a disturbing dream that God was defecating on the great towers of the Basel Cathedral.[75] As the son of an Evangelical Church pastor, Jung was terrified and deeply disturbed by this dream. Years later he concluded that the same institutionalized God to whom his father had consigned his life had intended the child to learn that his journey would not be like that of his father. Thus, from a sacred turd, so to speak, Jung would recover direct

---

[74] "Crucial Points in Psychoanalysis," *Freud and Psychoanalysis*, CW 4, par. 606.
[75] See *Memories, Dreams, Reflections*, pp. 36ff.

access to the divine through the power of dreams.

Years later, in a 1939 speech to the Guild for Pastoral Psychology in London, Jung would remind his clerical audience that they had too often substituted the buffer of institutional life for the reality of the spirit. Our ancestors, he noted, knew that the silence is not silent, that the darkness is luminous. For those who wait upon it, the sacred speaks through the activation of those inner imagos that link us to Mystery once again. Our ancestors knew this, which is how they were personally transformed, and subsequently transmitted their visions to the tribe. When the tribe formalized those visions by way of dogma and ritual practice, they forgot that if religious experience is not direct and personal, it is someone else's experience. Too often institutions have substituted prescribed ritual for the immediacy of religious encounter. As Jung reminds us,

> A creed is a confession of faith intended chiefly for the world at large and is thus an intramundane affair, while the meaning and purpose of religion lie in the relationship of the individual to God (Christianity, Judaism, Islam) or to the path of salvation and liberation (Buddhism).[76]

Like the memory of the childhood dream, Jung's encounter with the Mystery was experiential. "I don't *believe*," he wrote, "but I do *know* of a power of a very personal nature and irresistible influence. I call it 'God.' "[77] Such an encounter with the otherness of the Other constitutes the reality of transcendent connection which we claim to seek. As personal as this experience may be, its ultimate contribution is its power to link the alienated individual to the timeless journey of soul. As each person is the genetic carrier of the religious process, so the uniqueness of individual experience contributes to the richness of the collective encounter with Mystery. Rather than enforce uniformity, religious life needs to be individualized, not only to allow for the variety of experience, but also to contribute to the differentiated exfoliation of the Mystery.

---

[76] "The Undiscovered Self," *Civilization in Transition,* CW 10, par. 507.
[77] *Letters,* vol. 2, p. 274.

Spirituality and Soul

We are now obliged to exercise primary responsibility for our spirituality. Three indices are useful in helping define our relationship to that Cosmic Other.

First, there is the principle of *resonance*. Since the energy of soul is invisible, we can only track its movement as it momentarily incarnates in images.[78] The image may be an affect (an emotional state, such as panic where the god Pan is suffered), a physical sensation (a bodily state which carries both the wound and the desire of soul to heal), a dream (which presents itself out of the autonomous activity of the unconscious), or some external phenomenon, be it burning bush or a rock star. Certainly the grand religious traditions have preserved myriad images, some of which still carry the energy of soul for certain individuals. Each of us must sort through the magnificent ruins and find those images that speak to us, those that are personally resonant. Activation of the psychic tuning fork within tells us that soul is present. Like calls to like. The principle of resonance tells us what is of us, about us, for us, even as it retains its mystery. No effort of ego, however, can endow an image with mystery once mystery has fled.

The second test of our spirituality may be found in our encounter with *depth*. Whatever pulls us deeper into life, even painfully so, opens us to the great life that courses beneath history and below the surface of everyday appearance.[79] Soul is epiphenomenal; it is omnipresent and contiguous with all experiences of the phenomenal. To be pulled into the depths through our encounter with the Beloved, to encounter the depths within ourselves, to experience the awe of Nature, is truly to have a religious experience. To glimpse the invisible world that animates the visible one is to experience the Mystery that enlarges consciousness.

---

[78] See my *Tracking the Gods* for a more complete account of this task.

[79] In *Swamplands of the Soul*, I discuss at length how the invitation to the enlargement of soul may be found even in the darker states, such as depression, betrayal, loss and fear.

The third principle is *numinosity*. When Mystery winks at us, we realize that soul is not only in us, but also in the outer world. That glimmer is the autonomy of soul in the world which seeks to connect with us. Its movement may be seen in the epiphany of natural events, ranging from the course of the planets to the microscopic dance of life. It is found in the patterns of history, the frenzies of popular fevers, and in the daily encounter with others. The Hindu tradition of greeting by clasping the hands and bowing is an affirmation that one recognizes the presence of soul in the Other, and honors it.

These three modalities, then—resonance, depth and numinosity—are the primary indices of the presence of that autonomous Other which we call soul. We have been brought into life equipped to be the carriers of soul, recipients of soul and builders of soul. If there is another world, it is this one.

Those fortunate enough to live in a society where resonant images connect the tribe and the individual to the precincts of Mystery—cosmos, nature, tribal others—experience a psychic connection to the Other, and a sense of self grounded in a transcendent order. Those images are conduits into the natural world, with its specific tribal mythos, and assist in later moving the community members into a world beyond mortality. Moreover, such images conduct them through the developmental stages of life, rendering understandable and acceptable the various deaths and rebirths which constitute the path of maturation. Most of all, they are blessed to feel a sense of spiritual home in a world full of unending grief. As an anonymous Chippewa fragment had it:

> Sometimes I go about pitying myself,
> and all the time
> I am being carried by great winds across the sky.[80]

Those "great winds" are the movements of soul through history, and through the sensibility of the individual.

---

[80] Robert Bly, James Hillman and Michael Meade, *The Rag and Bone Shop of the Heart: Poems for Men*, p. 496.

For most of us, alas, there is no sense of being carried by those powers. Yet it was Jung, more than any other figure in our age, who taught that those same "great winds" still course through each of us.[81] He reminded us that the source of those unifying images which animated our ancestors and linked them to Mystery were generated by the symbol-making function we all possess. The same mysterious place whence come our dreams also births those mediating images which arise when we encounter the mysterious Other.

Archetypally speaking, the god-image emerges from our own depths. A god is defined then as an affectively charged image that emerges out of our encounter with Mystery. Such images are numinous; they wink at us and activate a resonant response. They are Wholly Other, for we cannot command them. They are inexplicable for they are experiential more than cognitive. They link us to largeness. And they constellate in us all sorts of metaphoric associations. Thus the death of a princess, for instance, is more than the loss of one person, more than a reminder of mortality; it activates a very wide range of associations, and occasions resonance at very deep levels across disparate human boundaries.

As we know, imagos that express the deep movement of soul can also reify, grow brittle, even die. We need to remember that the image is not the god; rather, it is the vehicle of the godly. It seems the common temptation of us all to adore the image rather than the Mystery to which it points. Such a mistaken relationship becomes the sin of idolatry, arising out of our anxious attempt to freeze, to hold on to, the Mystery. When we seek to fix it on behalf of the nervous ego's desire for security, we blaspheme, for we are seeking to limit the autonomy of Mystery. This is like trying to order up a certain kind of dream, or seeking to constrain its meaning.

I recall an analysand who came every week with a beautifully written essay that analyzed her dreams and tied up their meaning

---

[81] We should not be surprised by this notion, given that the various words for soul and spirit, such as *psychein, esprit, ruach, spiritus, anima, inspiration, respiration,* all embody the idea of "breath" as their central metaphor.

very neatly. When she was invited to consider another reading of a dream, she grew agitated and defensive. She was seeking to control the Mystery within, lest its autonomy threaten her fragile ego.

So we blaspheme when we seek to worship the image, control the god, manage the Mystery. This human tendency may be seen not only in religious institutions but in our ordinary desire to control our psychic processes rather than attend them, be charged by them and grow through the dialogue with them. That Other we seek "out there" is also the Other "in here."

The reification of an image through history, or through our own desire to fix its meaning in forms convenient to ego, leads to this peculiar oxymoron called "the death of God." How can a god, immortal by definition, die? What dies is rather the power of the image to point beyond itself toward the Mystery it once intimated. The idolatry of image occurs after the energy has already gone elsewhere. After the Crucifixion, the followers of Christ found his tomb empty. What his energy incarnated was no longer to be found in corporeal form, but in the activation of their archetypal encounter with Mystery. Fundamentalism and literalism are in the end soul denying. When the energy of soul has gone elsewhere, what is left are merely cultural artifacts, relics, graves. The image is, after all, only the husk which the Mystery once animated. To worship the husk makes no sense, yet the reification of historically charged images is why many of us can no longer connect with the Mystery.

It is important, then, to track the movement of soul as it appears, goes underground, and reappears in a new image. To hang on to the old image, when the godly is elsewhere, is not very religious after all, and not very smart. Not only institutional religion has committed this sin, but so has modern psychology. Ernest Becker wrote,

> All that psychology has accomplished is to make the inner life the subject matter of science, and in doing this, it dissipated the idea of soul. But it was the soul which once linked man's inner life to a transcendent scheme of cosmic heroism.[82]

---

[82] *Escape from Evil*, p. 97.

Becker's comment obliges us to realize that in literalizing the Mystery, we reduce it and ourselves. Our gods shrank because we were too small. To recover a right relationship to the gods, we must acknowledge their autonomy and see if we can follow their hermaneutic turns. As Jung noted, when the gods left Olympus they entered the gut, and their neglect now constitutes our sociopathies and our soul-disease:

> We think we can congratulate ourselves on having already reached such a pinnacle of clarity, imagining that we have left all these phantasmal gods far behind. But what we have left behind are only verbal spectres, not the psychic facts that were responsible for the birth of the gods. We are still as much possessed by autonomous psychic contents as if they were Olympians. Today they are called phobias, obsessions, and so forth; in a word, neurotic symptoms. The gods have become diseases; Zeus no longer rules Olympus but rather the solar plexus, and produces curious specimens for the doctor's consulting room, or disorders the brains of politicians and journalists who unwittingly let loose psychic epidemics on the world.[83]

Jungian psychology retains a sense of awe before the Mystery, and yet seeks a daily practice whereby one may track the gods and stand in relationship to the deepest mysteries of the Other. That Other is the animator of nature and the architect of our dreams— that which remains always beyond our powers to comprehend and contain. Were it otherwise, that Other would not really be Other, not really be the Mystery.

It is the tragedy of the Western world that the gods have gone underground. We all know this, yet fear to voice it. So we try to reinflate old images, finding ourselves still farther from Mystery. We desperately seek the gods, or, to assuage the pain of their loss, take refuge in phobias and addictions, dependence on others. We seek salvation through the aegis of a Magical Other. Yet, ironically, our lives often constitute a running away from the encounter with

---

[83] "Commentary on 'The Secret of the Golden Flower,' " *Alchemical Studies,* CW 13, par. 54.

the Other, whether by sabotaging intimate relationships or neglecting the invitation to consciousness. W. H. Auden observed,

> We would rather be ruined than changed.
> We would rather die in our dread
> Than climb the cross of the present
> And let our illusions die.[84]

Why? As the Twelve Step programs have it, "What we resist, will persist." Certainly the culprit is our omnipresent fear, which limits us and provokes the compulsion to repeat our same old patterns. "The spirit of evil," writes Jung, "is fear, negation, the adversary who opposes life in its struggle for eternal duration."[85] Only an existential courage can allow us to define ourselves, enlarge ourselves, in our relationship to the immensity of the universe.

Are we bold enough to live our journeys? Can we break through the imaginal frame of our acculturation and our complexes? Those are daunting questions, the answers to which define our psychic health. Here is how Jung put it in his autobiography:

> I have frequently seen people become neurotic when they content themselves with inadequate or wrong answers to the questions of life. They seek position, marriage, reputation, outward success or money, and remain unhappy and neurotic even when they have attained what they were seeking. Such people are usually confined within too narrow a spiritual horizon. Their life has not sufficient content, sufficient meaning. If they are enabled to develop into more spacious personalities, the neurosis generally disappears. For that reason the idea of development was always of the highest importance for me.[86]

Most of us, if we are honest, realize that we are confined within too narrow a spiritual horizon. There are certain questions we can then ask ourselves in order better to understand our situation:

1. If the central task of the first half of life is to build a solid ego identity, to leave Mom and Dad, go into the world of work and re-

---

[84] "The Age of Anxiety," in *Collected Poems,* p. 407.

[85] *Symbols of Transformation,* CW 5, par. 551.

[86] *Memories, Dreams, Reflections,* p. 140.

lationship and create a life, then what is the task of the second half
of life? What, indeed, is our proper vocation? If the first half of life
is about responding to what the world asks of us, then the task for
the second half is, what does the soul ask?

2. What is the unlived life that haunts us, summons us, judges
us? We all know, and yet daily deflect the question. We wait as if
someone else knows the answer and will offer it to us. No one else
knows what is right for us—not cleric, not parent, not partner, not
therapist—but something in us certainly knows, and through our
symptomatology expresses its dismay at our disregard.

3. Where are we stuck in our developmental process? What fears
intimidate us? Are they not the relics of childhood, the recollection
of wounding, of feeling abandoned or overwhelmed? Does not our
tacit collusion with those fears keep us walled up in the behaviors
of childhood?

4. Where do we lack permission to be ourselves? Where did we
lose the passion through which our nature seeks its own fullest expression? Where were we inadequately supported, discouraged by
parents or teachers? Where did we have insufficient modeling of
the journey ahead? Whatever the fates imposed—permission, passion, programming—we are summoned to break through the old
paradigms, to risk all, to be worthy of the journey to which the gods
have summoned us.

5. How do we define, practice, integrate our spirituality? Unless
our spirituality is more consciously evolved, we will lead superficial lives governed by routine, addictive behavior or collusion with
the collective. Our spirituality is the most critical field of relationship, for from the quality of our spirituality comes the tenor and
outcome of all other relationships.

We do know, intuitively, the answers to these questions, for all
are defined daily by the teleology of our own nature. Something in
us always knows, though we may not know what we know, may
fear what we know, or, like the old story of the encounter with
Death in Teheran, may flee that which is already with us and seeks

our acknowledgment.[87] To live these questions is what will define
our spirituality, our relationship to Mystery. We are asked to risk
largeness, passion, boldness, loneliness, and finally to risk being
what we were intended by the gods to be.

Three Poets Who Walked with the Gods

Ernest Becker's indictment of modern psychology, noted a few
pages back, is on target. It is a modern tragedy that clergy have forgotten the psyche, forgotten that religious experience must be personal to be real. And psychologists have forgotten soul, the mean-
ing-seeking, symbol-making Mystery which is our deepest reality.
Other than in the work of Jung and his followers, one is better ad-
vised to turn to the modern poet for clues as to the presence of soul.

In general, the central project of modern and post-modern lit-
erature has been to witness the dismantlement of the old hierarchi-
cal institutions on the one hand, and the difficulty of living without
connective mythos on the other. Thus one may often learn more of
the modernist spiritual dilemma from the artist, who limns the soul
in its deepest precincts, than from cleric or clinician.

Of the many eloquent voices on this modernist dilemma, I am
drawn most to three poets, Wallace Stevens, Hart Crane and Rainer
Maria Rilke. The oeuvre of each is a study in itself and represents a
profound religious sensibility, though most often expressed through
secular metaphors. (I could include Yeats, Eliot and many others.)

Wallace Stevens

Wallace Stevens imagines a woman who sits with her newspaper
and coffee on a Sunday morning.[88] A part of her muses on the images of her childhood,

---

[87] A laborer comes to his Master in a panic. "Oh, Master," he pleads, "let me flee
to Teheran, for I just met Death in the vineyard." The Master grants permission,
and later that day runs into Death himself. "Why did you frighten my servant?" he
asks Death. Death replies, "I only expressed my surprise that he was still here,
when we have an appointment to meet tonight in Teheran." (Source unknown)
[88] "Sunday Morning," in *Norton Anthology of Poetry,* p. 929.

> . . . over the seas, to silent Palestine,
> dominion of the blood and sepulchre.

Yet the poet asks why she should give her soul to images which now are dead for her.

> What is divinity if it can come
> only in silent shadows and in dreams?

Divinity, he concludes, "must live within herself." Stevens believes that divinity is present, immanent, experiential, but no longer found in the husks which the gods have abandoned. He envisions:

> Supple and turbulent, a ring of men
> Shall chant in orgy on a summer morn
> Their boisterous devotion to the sun,
> Not as a god, but as a god might be,
> Naked among them, like a savage source.

The central thought in this poem is found in the line, "Not as a god, but as a god might be." This is a distinctly modern sensibility. The original experience of the mystery of nature would be, in the animistic phase of civilization, embodied directly as divine. Later, that divine energy leaves the husk and the celebrant feels abandoned. Stevens, however, as a post-Kantian, post-Nietzschean, believes that one can phenomenologically experience the divinity of this world, but can only express such experience through conscious metaphors. Read it again and again, and feel it sink in: "Not as a god, but as a god might be."

This awareness of the metaphoric character of the image allows the poet to escape the literalism that is the trap of fundamentalism and psychosis. For Stevens, resonance, depth and numinosity are everywhere. His respect for the otherness of the Other obliges him to keep his "as if" structures conscious lest he limit the autonomy of that Other. This dilemma, then, replicates the task which we are to assume in intimate relationship as well. To allow the Other to be Other is not an easy task, but it is the only way to love them. This is true too of the gods, for we wish most from them.

Hart Crane

The concluding stanza of Hart Crane's magisterial "Voyages" is elliptical and profound. It does not lend itself to easy interpretation, or facile translation into prose.

> Bind us in time, O Seasons clear, and awe.
> O minstrel galleons of Carib fire,
> Bequeath us to no earthly shore until
> Is answered in the vortex of our grave
> The seal's wide spindrift gaze toward paradise.[89]

Crane asks not that we transcend this earthly state, but that we be bound in time, cast into this condition, with all the vicissitudes and changes of emotional seasons, and most of all with awe. Awe is acknowledged as the highest religious emotion. Awe is the proper experience of the other as truly Other. Every new parent has felt this awe. We have also been stunned this way when in the presence of the Beloved. And, even more, we stand with awe before the depth and breadth of the cosmos, acknowledging the largeness of that Cosmic Other.

The key metaphor of this Crane poem construes life as a voyage, and much of modernist testimony employs this archetypal idea. Since there is no longer any institution or world-view that is absolutely anchored, we experience ourselves as in exile and on a journey. In fact, one may say that the home of the modern is the journey itself. This home, this singing galleon on the high seas, is fired with the passions which fill our sails and drive us leeward. But Crane seeks no shore which is safe and secure; he wishes to remain on the high seas of the soul. If the journey is our home, then he would wish the journey to continue.

Where we are to arrive is intimated in the rich concluding line, "the seal's wide spindrift gaze toward paradise." This natural creature, as fleeting as we, is like a spindrift spray, yet stands open-eyed before the wonder and terror of the cosmos. It lives without know-

---

[89] Ibid., p. 1055.

ing, without certainty, gazing on the profound otherness of the
Other, gazing toward paradise. (I am reminded of John Keats's oft-
quoted observation: "Beauty is truth, truth beauty, that is all / Ye
know on earth, and all ye need to know.")[90] The radical willingness
to let be, rather than control, requires great courage and constitutes
the ultimate respect for the Mystery.

Rainer Maria Rilke

In my view, the artist who has most deeply plumbed the modern
spiritual condition is Rainer Maria Rilke. So many of his poems
testify to the terrible beauty of not knowing. He consistently refuses
to name, tie down or reify the mystery of the Other, whether that
other be one's lover or the gods. Of his many poems one could cite,
the following is suitably representative.

> Now it is time that gods came walking out
> of lived-in Things . . .
> Time that they came and knocked down every wall
> inside my house . . .
>   O gods, gods!
> who used to come so often and are still
> asleep in the Things around us, who serenely
> rise and at wells that we can only guess at
> splash icy water on your necks and faces . . .
> Once again let it be your morning, gods.
> We keep repeating. You alone are source.
> With you the world arises, and your dawn
> gleams on each crack and crevice of our failure.[91]

Myth is the invisible plane which supports visible conscious life.
When we experience its presence, we feel grounded, connected. But
if the Other World is really this one, then our spiritual sense needs
tuning. Surrounded by artifacts, by illusory and seductive sirens of
popular culture, our task is to intuit the presence of the gods, to lift
soul up and out of that delusory surface texture.

---

[90] "Ode on a Grecian Urn," ibid., p. 664.
[91] ""Now It Is Time that Gods Came Walking Out," in *Ahead of All Parting: The Selected Poetry and Prose of Rainer Maria Rilke,* p. 193.

The gods are always there, though we may not see them. Jesus said, "The kingdom of God is spread all over this earth and men do not see it."[92] Just so, that for which we search is already here, hiding in the depths, concealed by the superficial. The gods emerge from behind the façade, from beneath the surface, for those who have eyes to see. Then they often unsettle, even overthrow, the attitudes of consciousness. They knock down our carefully constructed lives and blow us about. Anyone who has experienced the reality of the psyche knows full well the revolutionary power of those energies.

Who among us has not wondered where the gods are today? Why do they not appear in burning bushes, speak from whirlwinds, animate new prophets? But for Rilke the gods *are* present. They are still implicit in the depths of all things, always capable of stunning us awake. Jung once said,

> God is the name by which I designate all things which cross my willful path violently and recklessly, all things which upset my subjective views, plans and intentions and change the course of my life for better or worse.[93]

This is a profound description of the divine as that Cosmic Other with its own will and capacity to disrupt our conscious course.

Rilke's conclusion, a petitionary paean to the gods, is to elicit them once again, to draw them forth, to make conscious the depth encounter which they invite. They are the source of all things, including us, and may even be discerned at work in our failures, in our frailty, and in our faulty comprehension. As the energy of the cosmos, the Primal Other, they are the powers which shake the soul into enlargement.

These brief excerpts represent but a fraction of the vast expression of soul-search in our time. These poets found themselves without the comforts of a tribal mythos, without the anchoring stability of institutions, and without the spiritual longitudes and latitudes with which to make their course chartable and their passage pre-

---

[92] *The Gospel According to Thomas,* 80:14.
[93] Interview in *Good Housekeeping,* December 1961.

dictable. Cast on the high seas of the soul, alone, they learned to value that journey as their home. They rejected the desire for dogma, the seductive impulse to encapsulate the Mystery by reason. They preferred the ambiguity of metaphor, its pointing beyond itself, to those fatuous certainties which force the gods into hiding.

As we saw earlier, Freud denigrated the religious impulse as a regressive desire to control the universe (and we do have that motive) and to find a good, omnipotent parent to protect us (and we have that motive too). But Jung understood that beneath these universal infantile desires lies something profound: the desire to render meaningful our brief earthly transit. In the excerpts above, these poets chose not to parentify the universe. They found the courage to allow the Other to be radically Other. Their vision provided them no comfort, no security, but gave them dignity and meaning. Their accounts of our contemporary dilemma were not regressive, as Freud predicted, but rather plunged them deeper into life, deeper into a respectful relationship with the Mystery.

There is a word that describes this attitude of respect for the Other, and it is *awe*. There is a word for that posture in which one stands awash in ambiguity and affirms it, and that word is *courage*. There is a word for that experience of reverence for the otherness of the Other, and that word is *love*.

> Last night, as I was sleeping,
> I dreamt—marvelous error!—
> that it was God I had
> here inside of my heart.[94]
>
> *
>
> When you really look for me, you will see me instantly—
> you will find me in the tiniest house of time . . .
> Student, tell me, what is God?
> He is the breath inside the breath.[95]

---

[94] Anthony Machado, "Last Night, As I Was Sleeping," in Bly, *The Soul Is Here for Its Own Joy*, p. 253.

[95] Kabir, "Breath," ibid., p. 88.

Afterword
The Two Insomnias

When I am with you, we stay up all night.
When you're not here, I can't go to sleep.
Praise God for these two insomnias!
And the difference between them.
—Rumi.

Early on I warned the reader how disappointing my words might be, how I do not like their premises myself. Perhaps their only virtue is that despite our hearts' desire they are valid. The evidence is strong that there are no Magical Others, that we befoul our relationships with our own psychic debris, that the best relationship we can ever achieve with the intimate Other, the corporate Other, and the Wholly Other, is a function of the relationship we achieve to ourselves. If all that is true, and I believe it is, then the most loving thing we can do for those we claim to love, and for the world, is to withdraw our projections and consciously assimilate them into our personal journey. But who wants to hear that?

So, go ahead, say that all this is too intellectual, too rational, too demanding, too cynical, even elitist. Cite the words of the seventeenth-century philosopher Blaise Pascal, that the heart has reasons that reason knows not. And you will be perfectly correct, and very much in the majority.

Once, after a seminar on relationship, a lovely lady brought me a greeting card. On the cover was pictured an ebullient cartoonish woman, smiling, gesticulating with one hand and holding a cup of coffee in the other, saying:

I don't need any man in my life to show me who I am, or to fill any empty voids. I am independent and strong. I don't need anyone as an emotional crutch to get me through life. I am as an island unto myself, providing all that I need for a happy, fulfilled life. I am at one with myself and the universe.

Inside the card was the single line, "God, am I lonely!"

And recall the sign above the desk of the Administrator of the Jung Foundation of Ontario: "The inner marriage is all very well, but it doesn't warm my feet at night."

A lady in New Jersey approached me after a talk on relationship, literally shaking her fist. "I agree with everything you said, but I still believe in love." I searched my memory for any comments I had made that might be construed as inimical to love. As a matter of fact, I am rather in favor of love, and certainly, as I trust is clear to those reading these words, in favor of clearing out some of the obstacles to the experience of it. I suspect that I had somehow gored the sacred romantic cow, the projective cow, the Magical Other cow, and I would not be forgiven that transgression.

Well, you may ask, is there any place, any legitimacy at all, for human need, compassion, empathy? Yes, surely. It is a healing gift to feel compassion for our partners in their moments of pain, to give them grounds for constancy and trust when their history has betrayed them, to encourage them along the perilous path beside our own. Certainly, as fragile, finite beings we are always vulnerable, at the mercy of an unpredictable universe, needful and desirous of surcease. Such desires are profoundly human and always present. When, however, they unconsciously dominate our behavior, we will be stuck in dependencies and regressive moves that ultimately serve not our developmental potential, nor the partner pressed to serve our needs, and not the society whose health depends on evolved adults.

I greatly value the work of those who practice couple therapy. I know they do much good work with many fractured relationships. Any healing in this area is to be celebrated. At the same time, I sense a secret or implicit fantasy beneath the exchanges partners are often encouraged to make, namely that the Other will somehow help to heal our oldest wounds. It is the same old, same old, recurring fantasy of the Magical Other, tough to shake. While it is helpful to bring to the surface the needs of each, I would suggest that then we know, as individuals, what our work is. And such work, to finally become responsible for ourselves, is onerous indeed.

In no way are these thoughts a denigration of the value of relationship. We need others to relate to, to reflect us back to ourselves, as others similarly need us. Jung, as always, has something important to say on the subject:

> The unrelated human being lacks wholeness, for he can achieve wholeness only through the soul, and the soul cannot exist without its other side, which is always found in a "You." Wholeness is a combination of I and You, and these show themselves to be parts of a transcendent unity.[96]

An explanatory footnote to the above passage reads as follows:

> I do not, of course, mean the synthesis or identification of two individuals, but the conscious union of the ego with everything that has been projected into the "You." Hence wholeness is the product of an intrapsychic process which depends essentially on the relation of one individual to another. Relationship paves the way for individuation and makes it possible, but is itself no proof of wholeness.[97]

Jung's observation seems simple enough, but there are nuances worth exploring. If we live a solitary life, isolated from others, then in the end we can come to believe that the whole cosmos is only what we think it to be. This is the universal human temptation, the timeless seduction, of anthropomorphism, ethnocentrism and egocentrism: the universe extends only as far as my nose. But when the Other insists on being Other, then my ego-centered view of the world is challenged. If I do not deny or withdraw, then I am obliged to enlarge my sense of reality. As great as the gift of caring and compassion may be, the ultimate gift to any relationship is the willingness to dialogue with the Other, which, in turn, can lead to individual enlargement. Dialogue with the Other, however unpleasant or painful, is the catalyst for individuation.

At the same time, Jung would value the inner tension of oppo-

---

[96] "The Psychology of the Transference," *The Practice of Psychotherapy*, CW 16, par. 454.
[97] Ibid., note 16.

sites and insist on the radical significance of the encounter with the Other within, the dialogue between ego and history, between ego and complex, between ego and Self. Just as there is a requisite encounter between ego and world whereby we form relationships with parents, with peers, with institutions, so there is an obligatory meeting with that Other we also are—the Other which seems both foreign and familiar, the Other which knows us and more than us, which fashions our dreams, our affects, our symptomatology.

As people undertake this inner dialogue, in therapy, in active imagination, in dream work, they come to know more of this Other. In time they may even come to trust that this Other, which they also are, sometimes knows what is best for them.

The goal of all life, be it the rhizome which seeks to become the leafy plant, or the embryo which seeks to become the soul-carrying individual, is wholeness. Wholeness, Jung clearly says in the above passage, is always contingent upon the dialogue of opposites, an I and a You. When we recognize the sacred value of the Other, be it another person or a part of oneself, then that You also becomes a Thou. Recall the two admonitions that graced the outer and inner entrances to the Oracle of Apollo at Delphi: "Know Thyself," and "Thou Art." These separate realities are paradoxically revealed to be aspects of the same thing. No matter how opposite are the opposites—mind and body, male and female, human and god—to experience them as aspects of an enlarged, single reality is to experience wholeness. And the intimation of wholeness, however transient, is ultimately religious, for therein one experiences the connectedness which honors opposites and yet knows transcendence.

Such momentary glimpses of wholeness, whether by way of the Beloved or the Cosmic Other, lie beyond the powers of pure reason. Only symbols, metaphors and images pointing beyond themselves to the ineffable can begin to communicate the experience. This symbolic epiphany is why the gods arise from the strangest places: in encounters with the Beloved, in solemn contemplation of eternity, in the excitement of a winning home-run, or in the evanescence of longing. When this transcendent unity is experienced, however fleetingly, we are what the gods intended—present to the Self. As the Self is the carrier of the sacred energy of the cosmos, at such moments we are also in the presence of the Divine. More than that cannot, and should not, be said.

Again, the poet offers us more assistance in moving through these realms than cleric or clinician. Like Stevens, Crane and Rilke, Toronto poet Kathie Wayne, in a poem titled "The Usual," tells us where the transcendent may be found:

> Do not think
> deities who walk, or angels
> their high wings heavy with wisdom
> are required for revelation,
> the usual will do.[98]

We might even then find the divine in our beloved Other, or in the dregs and dross of depression, or in the stunning encounter with the inner Other. Something ancient in us knows this, though we have forgotten. So Wayne reminds us:

> Any April, in a garden just
> your own, before they leave
> into green enormity of ears, and lean
> secret blushing stems to listen—
> listen: rhubarb shoots
> speak out, shout
> something you can't
> in the end pretend
> is news.

In my personal encounters with others I have been privileged, sometimes painfully, to grow. One such recent encounter came from my friend Peter Grant, who acquainted me with the thoughts of the priest Henri Nouwen. In *The Genesee Diary,* Nouwen recounts his seven-month stay in a Trappist monastery. He writes:

My first inclination has been, and in many ways still is, to connect love with something special in me that makes me lovable. When

---

[98] Correspondence with the author.

people are kind and friendly toward me, I feel happy because I think that they are attracted to me and like me in a special way. This more or less unconscious attitude got me in trouble here since the monk who is nice and good to me proves to be just as nice and good to everyone else. So it becomes hard to believe that he loves me because of anything special that I have and others do not have. . . .

It is important to me to realize how limited, imperfect, and weak my understanding of love has been. Not my theoretical understanding but my understanding as it reveals itself in my emotional responses to concrete situations. . . .

When we have found our own uniqueness in the love of God and have been able to affirm that indeed we are lovable since it is God's love that dwells in us, then we can reach out to others in whom we discover a new and unique manifestation of the same love and enter into an intimate communion with them.[99]

My friend Peter, also wrestling with the paradox of being loved versus being lovable, wrote as his commentary on Nouwen:

If I accept the fact that God loves me unconditionally, "no strings attached," I don't need to look to others for affirmation. I should be able to "be" myself and reach out and commune with that same love in others. . . . When this faith weakens it's then we begin to fall prey to the thinking that we really aren't lovable and we need to earn our love from others. If all love comes from God to begin with, it puts a whole different perspective on what it means to give and receive love from others.[100]

Peter is expressing the paradox that whatever the energy of love may be, it cannot be earned, cannot be coerced, cannot be controlled. Such energy may only be experienced, witnessed, shared. Such energy is "disinterested love," for it is not about engineering a particular, life-saving response from the Other. It allows the essence of the Other to *remain* Other. It does not oblige us to submit our separateness, our psychological integrity, to the Other in order to win something in return. It also allows us to be free.

But talk is cheap. The old agenda bubbles up. Rumi's twin in-

---

[99] *The Genesee Diary,* pp. 83f.
[100] From a letter to the author.

somnias trouble the night. It takes so damn much courage to be solely responsible for ourselves. And it is so often lonely.

For nearly a month the cardinal disappeared. I wondered if he had found a mate, or learned at last not to bash his head against glass walls. But no, he is back. Again, he flies several times a day against the transparent limits of desire. Perhaps one day he will learn not to be as foolish as us. Perhaps one day he will burst through that veil of illusion, the Maya, which seduces us all.

His work is ours; his suffering is ours; his longing is ours. Beneath the disparities which we are, we know ourselves to be this bird, and yet, besieged by the multiplicities of desire, we perforce must stand apart and suffer consciously, if only to bear witness to the immortal passion of his frail and hungry heart—and to our own.

Glossary of Jungian Terms

Amplification. A method of interpretation developed by Jung in which a dream image or motif is enlarged, clarified and given a meaningful context by comparing it with similar images from mythology, folklore and religion.

Anima (Latin, "soul"). The unconscious, feminine side of a man's personality. She is personified in dreams by images of females ranging from child to seductress to spiritual guide. A man's anima development is reflected in how he relates to women.

Animus (Latin, "spirit"). The unconscious, masculine side of a woman's personality. The animus is personified in women's dreams by images ranging from muscle-men to poets to spiritual leaders. A woman's animus development is reflected in how she relates to men.

Archetypes. Irrepresentable in themselves, archetypes appear in consciousness as images and ideas, universal patterns or motifs present in the collective unconscious. Archetypal images are the basic content of religion, mythology and art.

Complex. An emotionally charged group of ideas or images. At the core of a complex is an archetype or archetypal image.

Constellate. Whenever there is a strong emotional reaction to a person or a situation, a complex has been constellated (activated).

Ego. The central complex of consciousness. A strong ego can relate objectively to activated contents of the unconscious (i.e., other complexes) rather than identifying with them.

Feeling. One of the four psychic functions in Jung's model of personality types. (The others are thinking, sensation and intuition.) Feeling is the function that assesses the value of relationships and situations. It is different from emotion (affect), which results from the activation of a complex.

145

Individuation. The conscious realization of one's unique psychological reality, including both strengths and limitations. It leads to the experience of the Self as the regulating center of the psyche.

Participation mystique. A primitive, unconscious connection in which one cannot clearly distinguish oneself from other persons or sometimes even things. This is what lies behind the phenomena of identification and projection.

Persona (Latin, "actor's mask"). One's social role, derived from the expectations of society and early training. A persona is useful both in facilitating contact with others and as a protective covering, but identification with a particular persona (doctor, scholar, artist, etc.) inhibits psychological development.

Projection. A natural process whereby an unconscious characteristic of one's own is perceived in an outer object or person.

Self. The archetype of wholeness and regulating center of the psyche, experienced as a numinous power that transcends the ego (e.g., God).

Shadow. A mainly unconscious part of the personality, characterized by traits and attitudes, both negative and positive, which the conscious ego tends to reject or ignore.

Symbol. The best possible expression for something essentially unknown. Symbolic thinking is right-brain oriented, complementary to logical, linear, left-brain thinking.

Synchronicity. An acausal, meaningful coincidence between an event in the outside world and a psychological state.

Transcendent function. The reconciling new perspective which emerges from the unconscious (in the form of a symbol or a new attitude) after conflicting opposites have been consciously differentiated and the tension between them held.

Transference-countertransference. Particular cases of projection, used to describe the unconscious, emotional bonds that arise between two persons in a therapeutic relationship.

Bibliography

Auden, W.H. *Collected Poems.* New York: Random House, 1976.

Becker, Ernest. *Escape from Evil.* New York: MacMillan, 1985.

Bertine, Eleanor. *Close Relationships: Family, Friendship, Marriage.* Toronto: Inner City Books, 1992.

Bly, Robert, ed. and trans. *The Soul Is Here for Its Own Joy: Sacred Poems from Many Cultures.* Hopewell, NJ: Eco Press, 1995.

Bly, Robert; Hillman, James; and Meade, Michael, eds. *The Rag and Bone Shop of the Heart: Poems for Men.* New York: Harper Collins, 1992.

Buber, Martin. *I and Thou.* Trans. Walter Kaufmann. New York: Scribner, 1970.

Campbell, Joseph. *This Business of the Gods.* In Conversation with Fraser Boa. Caledon East, Ontario: Windrose Films, 1989.

Carotenuto, Aldo. *Eros and Pathos: Shades of Love and Suffering.* Toronto: Inner City Books, 1989.

Davis, Keith E. "Near and Dear: Friendship and Love Compared." In *Psychology Today,* vol. 19, no. 2 (Feb. 1985).

Dunn, Stephen. *New and Selected Poems, 1974-1984.* New York: W.W. Norton and Co., 1994.

Ellmann, Richard, and O'Clair, Robert, eds. *Modern Poems: An Introduction to Poetry.* New York: W.W. Norton and Co., 1976.

Faulkner, William. "A Rose for Miss Emily." In *Collected Stories.* New York: Random House, 1956.

Fitzgerald, Penelope. *The Blue Flower.* New York: Houghton-Mifflin, 1995.

Flores, Angel, ed. *An Anthology of German Poetry from Hölderlin to Rilke.* New York: Doubleday Anchor, 1960.

Freud, Sigmund. *The Future of an Illusion.* New York: W.W. Norton and Co., 1961.

The Gospel According to Thomas. New York: Harper and Brothers, 1959.

Hahn, Fred. "On Magic and Change." In *Voices,* October 1975.

Hanna, Edward. "The Relationship between the False Self Compliance and the Motivation to Become a Professional Helper." In *Smith College Studies in Social Work,* vol. 18, no. 3 (1990).

Hollis, James. *The Middle Passage: From Misery to Meaning in Midlife.* Toronto: Inner City Books, 1993.

_____. *Swamplands of the Soul: New Life in Dismal Places.* Toronto: Inner City Books, 1996.

_____. *Tracking the Gods: The Place of Myth in Modern Life.* Toronto: Inner City Books, 1995.

_____. *Under Saturn's Shadow: The Wounding and Healing of Men.* Toronto: Inner City Books, 1994.

Hopkins, Gerard Manley. *A Hopkins Reader.* Ed. John Pick. New York: Doubleday, 1966.

Horney, Karen. *Neurosis and Human Growth: The Struggle toward Self-Realization.* New York: W.W. Norton and Co., 1991.

Jacoby, Mario. *The Analytic Encounter: Transference and Human Relationship.* Toronto: Inner City Books, 1984.

Jung, C.G. *The Collected Works* (Bollingen Series XX). 20 vols. Trans. R.F.C. Hull. Ed. H. Read, M. Fordham, G. Adler, Wm. McGuire. Princeton: Princeton University Press, 1953-1979.

_____. *Letters* (Bollingen Series XCV). 2 vols. Ed. Gerhard Adler and Aniela Jaffé. Princeton: Princeton University Press, 1973.

_____. *Memories, Dreams, Reflections.* Ed. Aniela Jaffé. New York: Pantheon Books, 1961.

Kafka, Franz. *The Diaries of Franz Kafka, 1914-1923.* Trans. Martin Greenberg. Ed. Max Brod. London: Secker and Warburg, 1949.

Kean, Sam, and Valley-Fox, Anne. *Your Mythic Journey.* Los Angeles: Jeremy P. Tarcher, Inc., 1989.

Kunkel, Fritz. *Selected Writings.* Ed. John Sanford. Mahwah, NJ: Paulist Press, 1989.

Lackie, Bruce. "The Families of Origin of Social Workers." In *Clinical Social Work Journal,* vol. 32, no. 1 (1983).

MacLeish, Archibald. *Poems, 1924-1933.* New York: Houghton-Mifflin, 1933.

The Norton Anthology of Poetry. Ed. Alexander Alison et al. 3rd ed. New York: W.W. Norton and Co., 1970.

The Norton Introduction to Poetry. Ed. J. Paul Hunter. New York: W.W. Norton and Co., 1991.

Nouwen, Henri. *The Genesee Diary.* New York: Doubleday, 1989.

Pascal, Blaise. *Pensées.* New York: E.P. Dutton and Co., 1958.

Plato. *The Republic.* 2nd. ed. Trans. Desmond Lee. Harmondsworth, U.K.: Penguin Books, 1974.

_____. *The Symposium.* Trans. W.R.M. Lamb. Loeb Classical Library. Cambridge, MA: Harvard University Press, 1961.

Qualls-Corbett, Nancy. *The Sacred Prostitute: Eternal Aspect of the Fem-inine.* Toronto: Inner City Books, 1988.

Riemann, Fritz. *Grundformen der Angst.* Munich: E. Reinhardt, 1977.

Rilke, Rainer Maria. *Ahead of All Parting: The Selected Poetry and Prose of Rainer Maria Rilke.* Trans. Stephen Mitchell. New York: Modern Library, 1995.

_____. *Duino Elegies.* Trans. C.F. McIntyre. Berkeley: University of California Press, 1963.

_____. *Rilke on Love and Other Difficulties.* Ed. John Mood. New York: W.W. Norton, 1975.

Sanford, John A. *The Invisible Partners: How the Male and Female in Each of Us Affects Our Relationships.* New York: Paulist Press, 1980.

_____. *The Man Who Wrestled with God.* Mahwah, NJ: Paulist Press, 1987.

Sharp, Daryl. *Getting To Know You: The Inside Out of Relationship.* Toronto: Inner City Books, 1992.

_____. *Jungian Psychology Unplugged: My Life As an Elephant.* Toronto: Inner City Books, 1998.

_____. *The Survival Papers: Anatomy of a Midlife Crisis.* Toronto: Inner City Books, 1988.

Tillich, Paul. *Dynamics of Faith.* New York: Harper and Row, 1956.

_____. *The Shaking of the Foundations.* New York: Charles Scribner and Sons, 1948.

von Franz, Marie-Louise. *Alchemy: An Introduction to the Symbolism and the Psychology.* Toronto: Inner City Books, 1980.

_____. *C.G. Jung: His Myth in Our Time.* Trans. William H. Kennedy. Toronto: Inner City Books, 1998.

_____. *Projection and Re-Collection in Jungian Psychology.* Trans. William H. Kennedy. La Salle, IL: Open Court, 1980.

_____. *Puer Aeternus: A Psychological Study of the Adult Struggle with the Paradise of Childhood.* 2nd ed. Santa Monica: Sigo Press, 1981.

Winnicott, Donald W. *The Maturational Process and the Facilitating Environment.* New York: International Universities Press, 1965.

Index

Also in this Series, by Daryl Sharp

Please see last page for discounts and postage/handling.

THE SECRET RAVEN
Conflict and Transformation in the Life of Franz Kafka
ISBN 978-0-919123-00-7. (1980) 128 pp. $25

PERSONALITY TYPES: Jung's Model of Typology
ISBN 978-0-919123-30-9. (1987) 128 pp. **Diagrams** $25

THE SURVIVAL PAPERS: Anatomy of a Midlife Crisis
ISBN 978-0-919123-34-2. (1988) 160 pp. $25

DEAR GLADYS: The Survival Papers, Book 2
ISBN 978-0-919123-36-6. (1989) 144 pp. $25

JUNG LEXICON: A Primer of Terms and Concepts
ISBN 978-0-919123-48-9. (1991) 160 pp. **Diagrams** $25

GETTING TO KNOW YOU: The Inside Out of Relationship
ISBN 978-0-919123-56-4. (1992) 128 pp. $25

THE BRILLIG TRILOGY:

1. CHICKEN LITTLE: The Inside Story *(A Jungian romance)*
ISBN 978-0-919123-62-5. (1993) 128 pp. $25

2. WHO AM I, REALLY? Personality, Soul and Individuation
ISBN 978-0-919123-68-7. (1995) 144 pp. $25

3. LIVING JUNG: The Good and the Better
ISBN 978-0-919123-73-1. (1996) 128 pp. $25

JUNGIAN PSYCHOLOGY UNPLUGGED: My Life as an Elephant
ISBN 978-0-919123-81-6. (1998) 160 pp. $25

DIGESTING JUNG: Food for the Journey
ISBN 978-0-919123-96-0. (2001) 128 pp. $25

JUNG UNCORKED: Rare Vintages from the Cellar of Analytical Psychology
Four Books. ISBN 978-1-894574-21-1/22-8.. (2008) 128 pp. each. $25 each

THE SLEEPNOT TRILOGY:

1. NOT THE BIG SLEEP: On having fun, seriously *(A Jungian romance)*
ISBN 978-0-894574-13-6. (2005) 128 pp. $25

2. ON STAYING AWAKE: Getting Older and Bolder *(Another Jungian romance)*
ISBN 978-0-894574-16-7. (2006) 144 pp. $25

3. EYES WIDE OPEN: Late Thoughts *(Another Jungian romance)*
ISBN 978-0-894574-18-1.. (2007) 160 pp. $25

Also in this Series, by Edward F. Edinger

SCIENCE OF THE SOUL: A Jungian Perspective
ISBN 978-1-894574-03-6. (2002) 128 pp. $25

THE PSYCHE ON STAGE
Individuation Motifs in Shakespeare and Sophocles
ISBN 978-0-919123-94-6. (2001) 96 pp. Illustrated $25

EGO AND SELF: The Old Testament Prophets
ISBN 978-0-919123-91-5. (2000) 160 pp. $25

THE PSYCHE IN ANTIQUITY
   Book 1: Early Greek Philosophy
   ISBN 978-0-919123-86-1. (1999) 128 pp. $25
   Book 2: Gnosticism and Early Christianity
   ISBN 978-0-919123-87-8. (1999) 160 pp. $25

THE AION LECTURES: Exploring the Self in Jung's *Aion*
ISBN 978-0-919123-72-4. (1996) 208 pp. 30 illustrations $30

MELVILLE'S MOBY-DICK: An American Nekyia
ISBN 978-0-919123-70-0. (1995) 160 pp. $25

THE MYSTERIUM LECTURES
A Journey Through Jung's *Mysterium Coniunctionis*
ISBN 978-0-919123-66-3. (1995) 352 pp. 90 illustrations $40

THE MYSTERY OF THE CONIUNCTIO
Alchemical Image of Individuation
ISBN 978-0-919123-67-6. (1994) 112 pp. 48 illustrations $25

GOETHE'S FAUST: Notes for a Jungian Commentary
ISBN 978-0-919123-44-1. (1990) 112 pp. $25

THE CHRISTIAN ARCHETYPE A Jungian Commentary on the Life of Christ
ISBN 978-0-919123-27-4. (1987) 144 pp. 34 illustrations $25

THE BIBLE AND THE PSYCHE
Individuation Symbolism in the Old Testament
ISBN 978-0-919123-23-1. (1986) 176 pp. $30

ENCOUNTER WITH THE SELF
A Jungian Commentary on William Blake's *Illustrations of the Book of Job*
ISBN 978-0-919123-21-2. (1986) 80 pp. 22 illustrations $25

THE CREATION OF CONSCIOUSNESS
Jung's Myth for Modern Man
ISBN 978-0-919123-13-7. (1984) 128 pp. 10 illustrations $25

Also in this Series, by Marie-Louise von Franz

AURORA CONSURGENS: On the Problem of Opposites in Alchemy
ISBN 978-0-919123-90-8. (2000) 576pp. **30-page Index** *Sewn* $50
A penetrating commentary on a rare medieval treatise, scattered throughout with insights relevant to the process of individuation in modern men and women.

THE PROBLEM OF THE PUER AETERNUS
ISBN 978-0-919123-88-5. (2000) 288pp. **11 illustrations** *Sewn* $40
The term *puer aeternus* (Latin, eternal youth) is used in Jungian psychology to describe a certain type of man or woman: charming, creative, and ever in pursuit of their dreams. This is the classic study of those who remain adolescent well into their adult years.

THE CAT: A Tale of Feminine Redemption
ISBN 978-0-919123-84-7. (1999) 128pp. **8 illustrations** *Sewn* $25
"The Cat" is a Romanian fairy tale about a princess who at the age of seventeen is bewitched—turned into a cat. . . . One by one von Franz unravels the symbolic threads.

C.G. JUNG: His Myth in Our Time
ISBN 978-0-919123-78-6. (1998) 368pp. **30-page Index** *Sewn* $40
The most authoritative biography of Jung, comprising an historical account of his seminal ideas, including his views on the collective unconscious, archetypes and complexes, typology, creativity, active imagination and individuation.

ARCHETYPAL PATTERNS IN FAIRY TALES
ISBN 978-0-919123-77-9. (1997) 192pp. *Sewn* $30
In-depth studies of six fairy tales—from Spain, Denmark, China, France and Africa, and one from the Grimm collection—with references to parallel themes in many others.

REDEMPTION MOTIFS IN FAIRY TALES
ISBN 978-0-919123-01-4. (1980) 128pp. *Sewn* $25
A nonlinear approach to the significance of fairy tales for an understanding of the process of psychological development. Concise explanations of complexes, projection, archetypes and active imagination. A modern classic.

ON DIVINATION AND SYNCHRONICITY
The Psychology of Meaningful Chance
ISBN 978-0-919123-02-1. (1980) 128pp. **15 illustrations** *Sewn* $25
A penetrating study of the psychological aspects of time, number and methods of divining fate such as the I Ching, astrology, Tarot, palmistry, dice, etc. Extends and amplifies Jung's work on synchronicity, contrasting Western attitudes with those of the East.

ALCHEMY: An Introduction to the Symbolism and the Psychology
ISBN 978-0-919123-04-5. (1980) 288pp. **84 illustrations** *Sewn* $40

Designed as an introduction to Jung's weightier writings on alchemy. Invaluable for interpreting images in modern dreams and for an understanding of relationships. Rich in insights from analytic experience.

Also in this Series, by James Hollis

THE MIDDLE PASSAGE: From Misery to Meaning in Midlife
ISBN 0-919123-60-0. (1993) 128pp. *Sewn* $25
Why do so many go through so much disruption in their middle years? Why then? What does it mean and how can we survive it? Hollis shows how we can pass through midlife consciously, rendering the second half of life all the richer and more meaningful.

UNDER SATURN'S SHADOW: The Wounding and Healing of Men
ISBN 0-919123-64-3. (1994) 144pp. *Sewn* $25
Saturn was the Roman god who ate his children to stop them from usurping his power. Men have been psychologically and spiritually wounded by this legacy. Hollis offers a new perspective on the secrets men carry in their hearts, and how they may be healed.

TRACKING THE GODS: The Place of Myth in Modern Life
ISBN 0-919123-69-4. (1995) 160pp. *Sewn* $25
Whatever our religious background or personal psychology, a greater intimacy with myth provides a vital link with meaning. Here Hollis explains why a connection with our mythic roots is crucial for us as individuals and as responsible citizens.

SWAMPLANDS OF THE SOUL: New Life in Dismal Places
ISBN 0-919123-74-0. (1996) 160pp. *Sewn* $25
Much of our time on earth we are lost in the quicksands of guilt, anxiety, betrayal, grief, doubt, loss, loneliness, despair, anger, obsessions, addictions, depression and the like. Perhaps the goal of life is not happiness but meaning. Hollis illuminates the way.

THE EDEN PROJECT: In Search of the Magical Other
ISBN 0-919123-80-5. (1998) 160pp. *Sewn* $25
A timely and thought-provoking corrective to the fantasies about relationships that permeate Western culture. Here is a challenge to greater personal responsibility—a call for individual growth as opposed to seeking rescue from others.

CREATING A LIFE: Finding Your Individual Path
ISBN 0-919123-93-7. (2001) 160pp. *Sewn* $25
With insight and compassion grounded in the humanist side of analytical psychology, Hollis elucidates the circuitous path of individuation, illustrating how we may come to understand our life choices and relationships by exploring our core complexes.

ON THIS JOURNEY WE CALL OUR LIFE: Living the Questions
ISBN 1-894574-04-4. (2003) 160pp. *Sewn* $25
This book seeks a working partnership with readers. Hollis shares his personal experience only so that we may more deeply understand our own. It is a partnership rich in poetry as well as prose, but most of all it reminds us of the treasures of uncertainty.

Studies in Jungian Psychology
by Jungian Analysts   Quality Paperbacks

Prices and payment in $US (except in Canada, and Visa orders, $Cdn)

Risky Business: Environmental Disasters and the Nature Archetype
Stephen J. Foster (Boulder, CO) ISBN 978-1-894574-33-4. 128 pp. $25

Jung and Yoga: The Psyche-Body Connection
Judith Harris (London, Ontario) ISBN 978-0-919123-95-3. 160 pp. $25

The Gambler: Romancing Lady Luck
Billye B. Currie (Jackson, MS) 978-1-894574-19-8. 128 pp. $25

Conscious Femininity: Interviews with Marion Woodman
Introduction by Marion Woodman (Toronto) ISBN 978-0-919123-59-5. 160 pp. $25

The Sacred Psyche: A Psychological Approach to the Psalms
Edward F. Edinger (Los Angeles) ISBN 978-1-894574-09-9. 160 pp. $25

Eros and Pathos: Shades of Love and Suffering
Aldo Carotenuto (Rome) ISBN 978- 0-919123-39-7. 144 pp. $25

Descent to the Goddess: A Way of Initiation for Women
Sylvia Brinton Perera (New York) ISBN 978-0-919123-05-2. 112 pp. $25

Addiction to Perfection: The Still Unravished Bride
Marion Woodman (Toronto) ISBNj 978-0-919123-11-3. Illustrated. 208 pp. $30

The Illness That We Are: A Jungian Critique of Christianity
John P. Dourley (Ottawa) ISBN 978-0-919123-16-8. 128 pp. $25

Coming To Age: The Croning Years and Late-Life Transformation
Jane R. Prétat (Providence) ISBN 978-0-919123-63-2. 144 pp. $25

Jungian Dream Interpretation: A Handbook of Theory and Practice
James A. Hall, M.D. (Dallas) ISBN 978-0-919123-12-0. 128 pp. $25

Phallos: Sacred Image of the Masculine
Eugene Monick (Scranton) ISBN 978-0-919123-26-7. 30 illustrations. 144 pp. $25

The Sacred Prostitute: Eternal Aspect of the Feminine
Nancy Qualls-Corbett (Birmingham) ISBN 978-0-919123-31-1. Illustrated. 176 pp. $30

Longing for Paradise: Psychological Perspectives on an Archetype
Mario Jacoby (Zurich) ISBN 978-1-894574-17-4. 240 pp. $35

The Pregnant Virgin: A Process of Psychological Development
Marion Woodman (Toronto) ISBN 978-0-919123-20-5. Illustrated. 208 pp. $30pb/$35hc

Discounts: any 3-5 books, 10%; 6-9 books, 20%; 10-19, 25%; 20 or more, 40% .

Add Postage/Handling: 1-2 books, $6 surface ($10 air); 3-4 books, $8 surface

($12 air); 5-9 books, $15 surface ($20 air); 10 or more, $15 surface ($30 air)

Visa credit cards accepted. Toll-free: Tel. 1-888-927-0355; Fax 1-888=924-1814.

INNER CITY BOOKS, Box 1271, Station Q, Toronto, ON M4T 2P4, Canada
Tel. (416) 927-0355 / Fax (416) 924-1814 / booksales@innercitybooks.net